Beginner's Guide to
QUILTMAKING

by Jeri Simon

Landauer Publishing, LLC

Beginner's Guide to
QUILTMAKING

by Jeri Simon

Copyright © 2015 by Landauer Publishing, LLC
Projects copyright © 2015 by Jeri Simon

This book was designed, produced, and
published by Landauer Publishing, LLC
3100 101st Street, Urbandale, IA 50322
www.landauerpub.com
515-287-2144   800-557-2144

President/Publisher: Jeramy Lanigan Landauer
Vice President of Sales and Administration: Kitty Jacobson
Editor: Jeri Simon
Art Director: Laurel Albright
Photographer: Sue Voegtlin

Library of Congress Control Number: 2015903331

ISBN 13: 978-1-93526-72-2

This book is printed on acid-free paper.

Printed in United States

10 9 8 7 6 5 4 3 2 1

TABLE OF CONTENTS

GETTING STARTED
basics and beyond

Perfection is great and an accurate 1/4" seam is very important, but for me quilting is a fun hobby that allows me to express my creative side.

In the following chapters, you will find all the basics you need to be successful in your quilting. Each section builds on the previous one and includes clear step-by-step instructions and large easy-to-follow photos. As you work your way through each section, you'll gain the skills and confidence needed to complete all the projects in the book. Before you know it, you'll be creating cherished keepsakes for friends and family.

Jeri

Getting Started

offers important information about the equipment and supplies you need to begin your quilting experience. Tips and suggestions on choosing fabric for your quilts are included as well. Be sure to read about the importance of creating a 1/4" seam guide before you begin sewing.

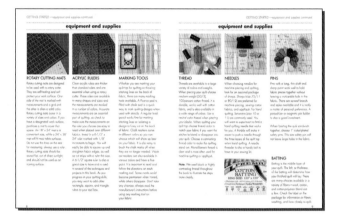

Quiltmaking Basics

teaches the techniques you need to know before beginning any quilt project. Start with rotary cutting lessons and various techniques to make quick work of half- and quarter-square triangle blocks. Instructions for sewing four-patch, pinwheel, and other basic blocks are included so you can practice your sewing skills. Lots of photos with step-by-step directions will guide you.

Tips

are sprinkled throughout each section and offer suggestions to help you be successful in your quilting. The tips are highlighted with a colored background.

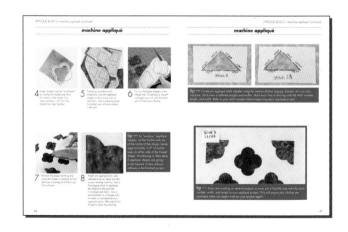

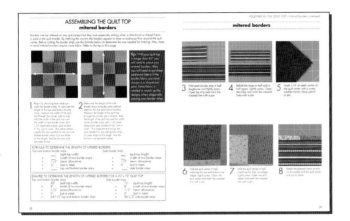

Assembling the Quilt Top

explains how to assemble a straight or diagonal-set quilt top with optional setting squares, sashing strips, and cornerstones. Borders are also part of the assembly process and full-color photos and instructions teach you how to add straight or mitered borders.

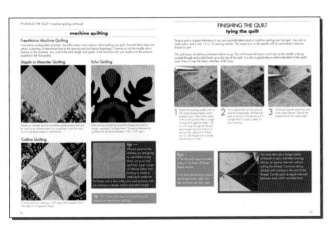

Finishing the Quilt

is the last step in the quilting process and is just as important as the first. Learn about layering the backing, batting, and quilt top. Various hand and machine quilting techniques are covered, as well as adding binding to complete your quilt.

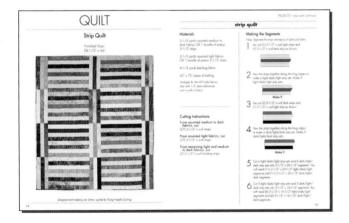

Projects

are included so you can immediately use the skills you have just learned to create your own quilt or table topper. The projects range in size from table toppers to a wallhanging to quilts—all of which can be created with the techniques you have just mastered.

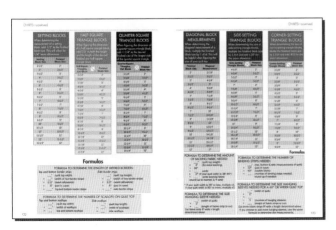

Charts

provide a quick reference when determining the measurements of diagonal blocks, side-setting and corner triangles, and half- and quarter-square triangle blocks. Also included are charts letting you know the number and sizes of squares and strips that can be cut from specific yardage. Formulas for determining the number of border and binding strips to cut for your quilt top are also in this section.

Getting Started

Elements of a Quilt Top

The main elements of a quilt are the quilt top, batting, and backing. These pieces are layered together and secured with machine stitching, hand stitching or tying. The quilt top is made up of blocks and borders in many combinations. Refer to pages 53-55 to see a variety of quilt top settings.

When you come across a word that is unfamiliar, refer to Quilting Terms & Definitions on pages 125-127. Many words and terms are unique to quilting and frequently used in patterns, books, and tutorials.

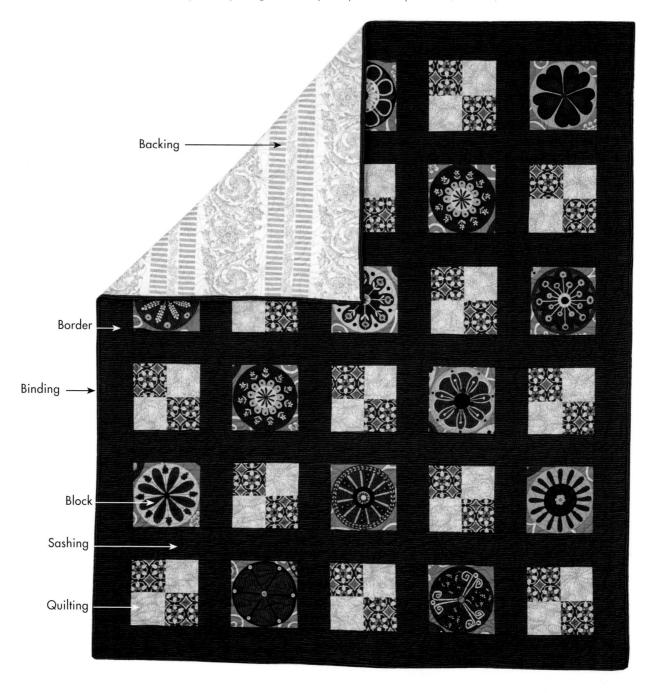

Backing

Border

Binding

Block

Sashing

Quilting

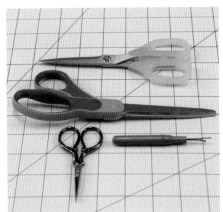

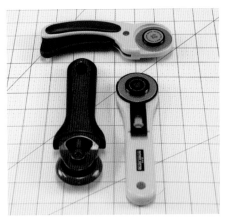

SEWING MACHINE

A sewing machine is an essential tool for almost every phase of quiltmaking. This doesn't mean you need to go out and buy a fancy new machine. All you need is a machine that sews an accurate 1/4" seam. If your machine hasn't been used for a while, take it to a professional to have it cleaned and checked over. If you are planning to purchase a new machine, one feature you will want to look for is the needle-down function. This function comes in handy when chain piecing patchwork, adding borders, or free motion quilting. Also, check to see if the machine comes with a walking foot. This foot is built in on some machines and available as an extra accessory on others.

SCISSORS

Sharp scissors in varying sizes will make it easier to snip threads and cut fabric. Purchase a quality pair of 8" fabric shears and keep a pair of small scissors by your sewing machine to cut threads. A medium-sized pair of scissors is handy for trimming fabric and block edges. You will also want to have a seam ripper on hand to undo any stitching mistakes.

ROTARY CUTTERS

Rotary cutters are designed to cut through more than one layer of fabric, which means their blades are extremely sharp. All are equipped with safety features, but if you have small children, invest in a cutter that features a safety lock and keep it out of reach.
Get in the habit of closing the cutter after each use. Rotary cutters are designed to be used on a rotary cutting mat. Do not use them on other surfaces. Purchase a rotary cutter with a 45mm blade to begin. It is a good size for any project. You can always add 60mm and 28mm rotary cutters to your sewing kit later.

equipment and supplies

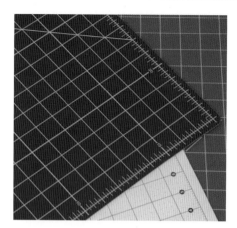

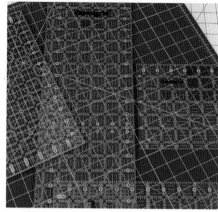

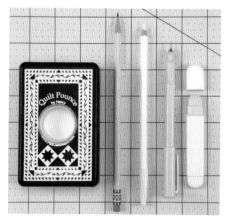

ROTARY CUTTING MATS

Rotary cutting mats are designed to be used with a rotary cutter. They are self-healing and will protect your work surface. One side of the mat is marked with measurements and a grid and the other is often a solid color. Rotary cutting mats come in a variety of sizes and colors. If you have a designated work surface, purchase a mat to cover that space. An 18" x 24" mat is a convenient size, while a 24" x 36" mat will fit most table surfaces. Do not use the lines on the mat for measuring; always use a ruler. Rotary cutting mats should be stored flat, out of direct sunlight, and should not be used as an ironing surface.

ACRYLIC RULERS

Clear acrylic rulers are thicker than standard rulers and are essential when using a rotary cutter. These rulers are available in many shapes and sizes and the measurements are marked in a number of colors. Accurate measurements are an essential part of quilting, so check to make sure the measurements on the ruler you choose are easy to read when placed over different fabrics. Invest in a 6-1/2" x 24" ruler marked with 1/8" increments to begin. You will easily be able to square up and straighten fabric edges, as well as cut strips with a ruler this size. A 6-1/2" square ruler is also a good size to have and is used in several of the techniques and projects in this book. As you progress in your quilting skills, you may want to add other rectangle, square, and triangle rulers to your tool box.

MARKING TOOLS

Whether you are marking your quilt top for quilting or drawing stitching lines on the back of fabric, there are many marking tools available. A Pounce pad is filled with chalk and is a quick way to mark quilting designs when used with stencils. A regular lead pencil works fine for marking stitching lines or isolating a design to fussy cut on the back of fabric. Chalk markers come in different colors so you can choose which will show up best on your fabric. It is also easy to brush the chalk marks off when they are no longer needed. Wash out markers are also available in various colors and have a fine point. It is important to read and follow the directions on each marking tool. Some marks could become permanent when ironed, while others disappear. Don't take any chances; always read the manufacturer's instructions before using any marking tool on your fabric.

equipment and supplies

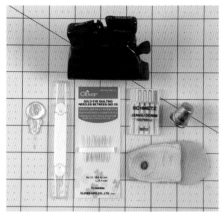

THREAD

Threads are available in a large variety of colors and weights. When piecing your quilt choose medium weight (50/3), 100-percent cotton thread. It is durable, works well with cotton fabric, and is also available in a wide range of colors. Use a neutral color thread when piecing your blocks. When quilting your quilt top choose thread color to match your fabric if you want the stitches to blend or disappear into your quilt. Choose a contrasting thread color to make the quilting stand out. Monofilament thread is clear and is most often used for machine quilting or appliqué.

Note: We used black or highly contrasting thread throughout the book to illustrate the steps more clearly.

NEEDLES

When choosing needles for machine piecing and quilting, look for an assorted package of sharps. Sharps (size 75/11 or 80/12) are preferred for machine piecing, sewing cotton fabrics, and appliqué. For hand quilting, betweens (size 10 or 11) are commonly used. You will want to experiment to find a hand quilting needle that works for you. A thimble will make it easier to push a needle through the three layers of the quilt top when hand quilting. A needle threader is also a handy tool to have in your sewing kit.

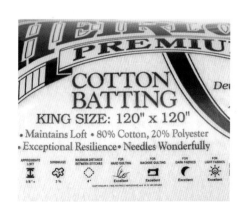

PINS

Pins with a long, thin shaft and sharp point work well to hold fabric pieces together without leaving a noticeable hole in the fabric. There are several brands and styles available and it is really a matter of personal preference. A pincushion or magnetic pin holder is also a good investment.

When basting the quilt sandwich together, choose 1" nickel-plated safety pins. This size safety pin will not leave large holes in the fabric.

BATTING

Batting is the middle layer of your quilt. The loft, or thickness, of the batting will determine how your finished quilt will lay. There are many choices available in a variety of fibers—wool, cotton, and cotton-polyester blend are a few. Check the label on the package for information on fibers, washing, and how closely to quilt.

9

GETTING STARTED
choosing fabrics

Choose fabrics that are 100-percent cotton when shopping for quilting fabric. Broadcloth weight cotton fabric, or quilting cotton, is easy to work with and durable. It also has a higher thread count which means less fraying and shrinkage. Fabric is sold by yardage and cut from a bolt or displayed in precut packs and sizes. Look for the ones listed below at your favorite fabric retailer.

BOLT

Fabric yardage is wrapped around and cut from a cardboard bolt. Information about the fabric, including fiber content, manufacturer's name, and care instructions, is found on the end of the bolt. Check to be certain the fabric you are buying is 100-percent cotton.

FAT QUARTER

18" x 22" piece of fabric

You'll find these displayed in a variety of ways at quilt shops. Fat quarters are a common requirement in quilt patterns.

A fat quarter is wider, but not as long as a quarter yard cut. Quarter yard cuts are 9" x width of fabric (generally 40"-44").

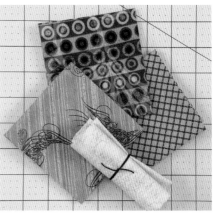

FAT EIGHTH

9" x 22" piece of fabric

These can be displayed in a variety of ways at quilt shops.

A fat eighth is wider, but not as long as an eighth yard cut. Eighth yard cuts are 4-1/2" x width of fabric (generally 40"-44").

2-1/2" STRIPS

These 2-1/2"-wide fabric strips are bundled in a variety of coordinating colors and patterns from the same fabric line. The name and number of strips varies by fabric line and manufacturer.

Common names: Jelly Roll, Roll Ups, Bali Pops, Rolie Polies, Pixie Strips, Tonga Treat Strips, Stone Strips, Strips

5" SQUARES

These 5" fabric squares are bundled in a variety of coordinating colors and patterns from the same fabric line. The name and number of squares varies by fabric line and manufacturer.

Common names: Charms, Bali Snaps, Tonga Treat Minis, 5" Stackers, Chips

10" SQUARES

These 10" fabric squares are bundled in a variety of coordinating colors and patterns from the same fabric line. The name and number of squares varies by fabric line and manufacturer.

Common names: Layer Cakes, Bali Crackers, Ten Squares, Patty Cakes, Tonga Treat Squares, 10" Stackers, Tiles

choosing fabrics

Additional Precut Fabric Bundles

- 2-1/2" squares - Candies, Mini Charms

- 5" x 44" strips - Dessert Roll, Twice the Charm, Fat Rolls, Charm Rolls

- 6" Hexagons - Hexies, Honeycombs

- 6" x 44" strips - Tonga Treats

TRIANGLES

These fabric triangles are bundled in a variety of coordinating colors and patterns from the same fabric line. The name, number and size of triangles varies by fabric line and manufacturer.

Common names:
Turnovers, HST (half-square triangles)

1-1/2" STRIPS

These 1-1/2" wide fabric strips are bundled in a variety of coordinating colors and patterns from the same fabric line. The name and number of strips varies by fabric line and manufacturer.

Common names: Honey Buns, Skinny Strips, Rolie Polies

FLANNEL FABRICS

Flannel fabrics are soft and make warm, cuddly quilts. Flannel can also be more challenging to work with than quilting cottons.

Flannel fabrics tend to shrink 2-5 percent more than regular cotton fabrics. It also frays when prewashed, so I don't prewash my flannel fabric. If you do choose to prewash, purchase extra yardage to allow for shrinkage and fraying. Flannels also tend stretch more easily, so use care when pressing and use a walking foot when piecing. Purchase quality fabric. Stay away from inexpensive, stretchy flannels.

Choose a pattern with large, simple pieces. Start with a new 80/12 needle. If you are working on a larger quilt, discard the needle when you are finished. Flannel tends to dull a needle more quickly than cotton. Use a 3/8" or 1/2" seam allowance on your flannel quilt instead of the normal 1/4" seam allowance. The seams will hold up better if fraying occurs. Clean your sewing machine often when working with flannel fabric. You'll be surprised at the amount of lint you remove.

Flannel fabrics are heavier than cotton, so use a low-loft batting. If you are using flannel on the front and back of the quilt, you may choose to eliminate the batting altogether.

color

Color is really a personal choice; there are no written rules when choosing colors for your quilt. Most people gravitate toward certain colors. Obviously, you don't want to use only one color in your quilt, so choose colors that complement each other. They don't need to match, they just need to blend. A color wheel can be helpful when choosing your quilt's color scheme.

Color Wheel

Warm Colors
Red, yellow, orange

Cool Colors
Blue, green, purple

value

The lightness or darkness of a color is referred to as value. Select fabrics in a variety of color values for your quilt. The value or contrast in the fabrics will clarify the design in your quilt and add depth to the pieced blocks. If you are choosing fabrics for a project from a book or magazine, the instructions will call for light, medium, or dark fabrics.

Light to Dark Values

Light to Dark Values

tip — When I have trouble telling if there is enough contrast between the fabrics I have chosen, I place the fabrics on a table or design wall and step back and squint my eyes. It allows me to determine if the colors are too similar and will look "mushy" in my quilt top. Taking a black and white digital picture or photocopy of the fabrics also shows if there is enough contrast.

color, value, and scale

scale

Scale refers to the size of the pattern or print of the fabric. Fabric patterns are described as small, medium, or large scale. Choose a range of small-, medium-, and large-scale prints in varying color values when designing your quilt top.

Small-scale prints look solid from a distance, but add texture and interest to the quilt top. These prints can also help calm down an otherwise busy quilt and give the eye a resting place.

Medium-scale prints retain their design when cut. They are a good choice for blocks, borders, and all elements of the quilt top.

Large-scale prints are best used for larger blocks or borders. Their design is often lost when cut into smaller pieces.

From left: small-, medium-, and large-scale prints

A focus fabric can serve as an inspiration when choosing fabrics for a quilt. Oftentimes, the focus fabric is simply used to pull colors together and is not actually used in the quilt. Choose a fabric you like with a pattern or variety of colors; this is your focus fabric. Pick additional fabrics in coordinating colors but with varying value and scale to complement the focus fabric. Be sure there is a variety of color, value, and pattern in your choices.

The focus fabric in the center of the collection is surrounded by a variety of complementary fabrics.

tip — A wide variety of fabric kits and patterns are available at most quilt shops. Begin with one of these kits until you are comfortable choosing fabrics on your own. Packs of fat quarters are also available and are a good starting place when choosing fabric color and scale.

GETTING STARTED
fabric grain

The fabric grain refers to the direction of the threads in the fabric. All woven fabrics have a lengthwise, crosswise, and bias grain. If a pattern instructs you to cut on the straight of grain it is referring to the lengthwise or crosswise fabric grain.

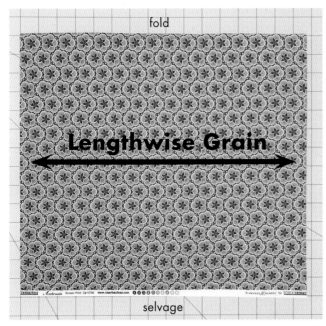

The lengthwise grain runs the length of the fabric and parallel to the selvage. It has the least amount of stretch and the greatest strength.

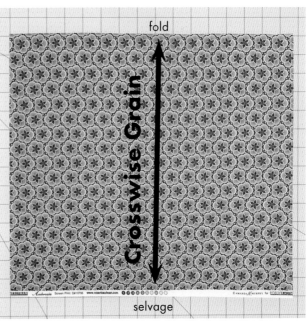

The crosswise grain runs perpendicular to, or between, the selvages. It has a bit more stretch than the lengthwise grain.

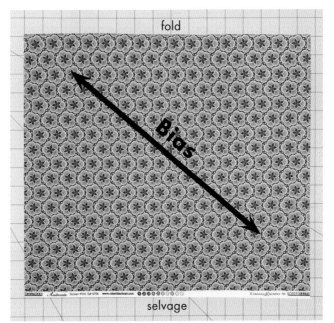

The bias is a fabric's 45-degree angle. It has the most stretch and has to be handled very carefully to avoid distortion in your quilt. Fabrics cut on the bias can be used for vines in appliqué or making curves.

Width of Fabric
WOF
measure from selvage to selvage

Width 2"

Selvages

Fold

GETTING STARTED
pressing

Pressing differs from ironing. Pressing is the motion of picking the iron up and putting it down on the fabric. Every seam needs to be pressed before adding another unit or block. Press the seam allowance toward the darker fabric whenever possible. The only time you will need to iron your fabric is after prewashing, if you choose to prewash, and before cutting.

When pressing a unit or block, press the seams from the back first. Press the stitched seam to embed the threads into the fabric. This action will also eliminate any puckers.

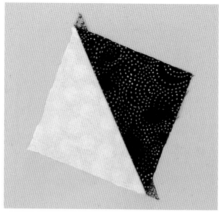

Turn the unit right side up and press the pieces open.

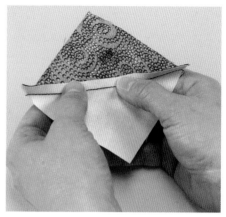

Finger-pressing can be used on smaller blocks to direct the seam allowance, but it is not a substitute for pressing with an iron. Finger-pressing is exactly what it sounds like; use your fingers to gently press the block pieces open from the back.

Turn the block to the right side and press your fingers along the seam allowance.

Pressing seams open may be necessary if several seams come together in one area. To press seams open, move your fingernail ahead of the iron to hold the seam allowance open.

Turn the unit over and press from the front. A pinwheel block is an example of when it may be necessary to press seams open.

tips —
- Refer to the manufacturer's instructions to remove any markings from your fabric before pressing. Heat from the iron could cause permanent markings on the fabric.
- Every quilter has different feelings about using steam when pressing. Personally, I only use steam after my block is complete. Experiment and see what works best for you, but remember to press not iron. If you iron while using steam you could distort your block.

Watch a demonstration of this technique at landauerpub.com/videos/fabricprep.html

GETTING STARTED
1/4" seams

An accurate 1/4" seam allowance is one of the most important aspects of quilting. If your seams aren't exact, your fabric pieces won't match up correctly and your points and corners won't fit together neatly.

laminated seam guide

Even if your machine has a 1/4" presser foot, it is wise to make a seam guide. Use the seam guide when piecing your quilts. It will assist you in creating perfect patchwork.

Make a laminated seam guide and tape it to your machine. Use the guide to line up your fabric pieces as you feed them under the presser foot.

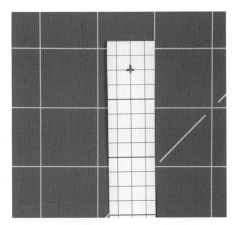

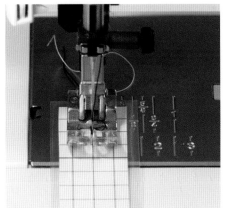

1 Cut a piece of 1/4" graph paper five lines wide and at least 6" long. Mark the graph paper with a "+" in the center of the top rectangle, as shown. Laminate the seam guide and cut out.

Note: If you don't have graph paper, copy the seam guide on page 19. Check the seam guide after copying to make sure the lines are exactly a 1/4" apart.

2 Place the seam guide under the needle on your machine and lower the needle into the center of the "+". Adjust the seam guide so the edge is parallel to the lines on the throat plate or presser foot.

3 Tape the guide in place on your machine, leaving the guide as long as possible. This will allow you to align the fabric correctly while feeding it under the needle. Trim the square with the "+" and the bottom portion of the seam guide that is not taped down. Raise the needle and remove the square with the "+".

Continue with Testing the 1/4" Seam directions on page 19.

> **tip** — Do not discard the square with the "+". You will need to reset the laminated seam guide any time you remove it from your machine. To reset it, place the "+" on the square under the needle and align the seam guide with it. Always retest your 1/4" seam.

graph paper

Use a rectangle of 1/4" graph paper and painter's tape to make a temporary seam guide. This will enable you to see where to align your fabric edge under the presser foot. You may choose to leave the tape on your machine as a permanent guide.

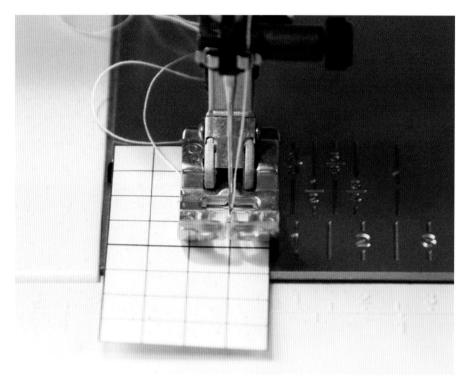

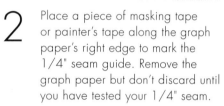

2 Place a piece of masking tape or painter's tape along the graph paper's right edge to mark the 1/4" seam guide. Remove the graph paper but don't discard until you have tested your 1/4" seam.

Continue with Testing the 1/4" Seam directions on page 19.

1 Cut a rectangle of 1/4" graph paper. Trim the graph paper along a grid line. Place the paper under the presser foot and lower the needle through the line closest to the trimmed right edge.

Watch a demonstration of this technique at landauerpub.com/videos/quarterinchseam.html

testing the 1/4" seam

After making your seam guide, test it to be certain the 1/4" seam mark is correct.

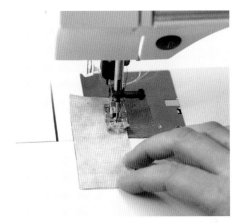

1 Cut three 1-1/2" x 3-1/2" rectangles of contrasting fabric. With right sides together, sew two of the strips together along the 3-1/2" side of the fabric using the 1/4" seam guide.

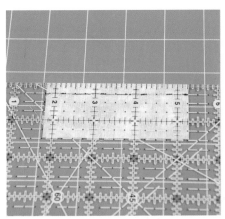

2 Measure between the raw edge of the fabric and the stitching line. The distance should be 1/4". If the seam does not measure 1/4", adjust your seam width and test again. Continue adjusting until you achieve a 1/4" seam.

3 Once the seam measures 1/4" sew the third 1-1/2" x 3-1/2" rectangle to the other two. Press the seam allowances away from the center strip.

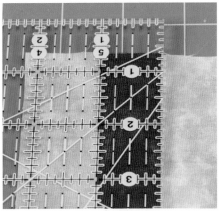

4 Measure the width of the center strip on the right side of the fabric. It should measure 1"-wide if the seam allowances are correct. The strip set should measure 3-1/2" x 3-1/2".

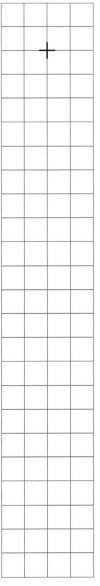

Seam Guide

Scant 1/4"

tip — Some quilt patterns and instructions require you to sew a scant 1/4" seam. This equals one or two thread widths inside the 1/4" seam mark.

QUILTMAKING BASICS

Quiltmaking Basics teaches the techniques you need to know before beginning any quilting project. Begin with rotary cutting lessons and move into chain piecing, fussy cutting, and stitching blocks.

rotary cutting

piecing

fussy cutting

strip piecing

sewing basic blocks

QUILTMAKING BASICS
rotary cutting

Straightening the Fabric

Fabric edges must be straightened before you begin to cut. It is important to start with a straight fabric edge, since the accuracy of your strips and squares are determined by the first cut.

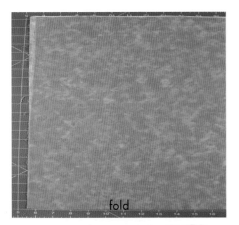

1 Fold the fabric in half, matching the selvages at the top. Place the fabric on the cutting mat keeping the selvages even and smoothing out any wrinkles. The fold should be closest to you.

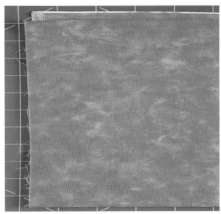

2 If you are working in a small space or on a small cutting mat fold the fabric again so there are four layers. Smooth out any wrinkles. The fold should be closest to you.

3 Place a 6-1/2" square ruler on top of the fabric, aligning one of the ruler's lines with the fabric's folded edge. Position a 6-1/2" x 24" ruler next to the square ruler so it lies just over the left raw edge.

4 Slide the square ruler away while keeping your left hand firmly on the rectangular ruler. The raw edge of the fabric should be under the rectangular ruler.

5 Hold the rotary cutter next to the right edge of the ruler and roll it away from you using a firm, downward pressure while cutting through the layers of fabric. As you cut through the fabric walk your fingers up the ruler. This allows you to keep pressure on the ruler, making it less likely to slip out of position.

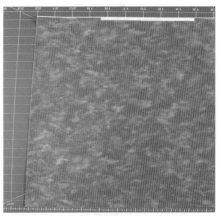

6 You now have a straight edge to begin cutting fabric strips. Be careful not to move the fabric or you may need to repeat the straightening process.

Watch a demonstration of this technique at landauerpub.com/videos/fabricprep.html

rotary cutting

Cutting Fabric Strips

Once your fabric has a straight edge you are ready to begin cutting strips.

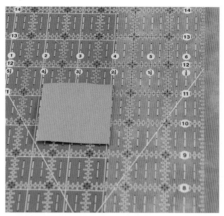

1 Determine the width of the strips needed. Our sample uses 2-1/2"-wide strips. Align the ruler's 2-1/2" marking with the straightened fabric edge. Applying pressure on the ruler with your left hand and beginning at the bottom fold, cut along the right edge of the ruler all the way to the selvages.

2 If your project calls for multiple strips of the same width, use a Post-it® note or masking tape on the ruler as a reminder of the measurement to cut.

tip — With your hand on the ruler, place your little finger on the cutting mat and butted up against the ruler when cutting your fabric. This helps to stabilize the ruler and prevent it from sliding on the fabric.

tip — Adhesive disks are available to place on the back of rulers to prevent them from slipping when cutting. Check with your local quilt shop for information on these products.

Cutting Wider Fabric Strips

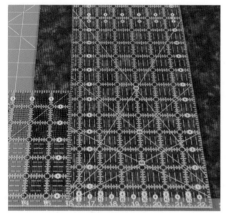

1 To cut wider fabric strips you may need to use two rulers. For example, to cut 8-1/2" -wide strips without access to an 8-1/2"-wide ruler, place a small ruler along the fabric's straight edge measuring in 2". Place the 6-1/2" x 24" ruler against the right edge of the small ruler. Together they total 8-1/2".

2 Cut along the right edge of the rectangular ruler to make an 8-1/2" strip. Walk your fingers up the ruler as you cut to hold it securely in place.

tip — It may be necessary to restraighten the fabric after cutting multiple strips.

Watch a demonstration of this technique at landauerpub.com/videos/fabricprep.html

rotary cutting

Subcutting Fabric Strips into Squares

When a project requires multiple squares or rectangles, cutting the shapes from strips makes the process go more quickly.

2 Determine the size of the squares needed. Align the straightened edge of the strip with the ruler marking that corresponds to the width of the square you wish to cut. Use a Post-It® note on the ruler as a reminder of the size of square to cut.

1 To cut squares from the fabric strips, place a folded strip on the cutting mat horizontally in front of you. Square-off the end of the strip and remove the selvages.

3 Cut the number of squares needed. Use the same process to cut multiple rectangles from fabric strips.

left-handed rotary cutting

Straightening the Fabric

If you are left-handed the steps for rotary cutting are the same; you just cut from the right side of the fabric instead of the left side. Since quilting is visual, especially for the beginner, photos of rotary cutting for the left-hander are provided.

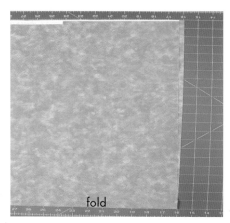

1 Following the same process on page 21, fold the fabric in half, matching the selvages at the top. Place the fabric on the cutting mat keeping the selvages even and smoothing out any wrinkles. The fold should be closest to you.

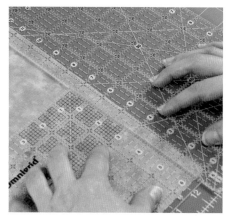

2 Place the 6-1/2" square ruler on top of the fabric, aligning one of the ruler's lines with the fabric's folded edge. Position the 6-1/2" x 24" ruler next to the square ruler so it lies just over the right raw edge.

3 Slide the square ruler away keeping your right hand firmly on the rectangular ruler. The raw edge of the fabric should be under the rectangular ruler.

4 Hold the rotary cutter next to the left edge of the ruler and roll it away from you using firm, downward pressure while cutting through the layers of fabric.

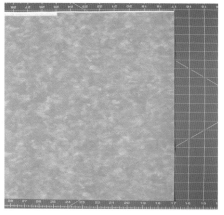

5 You now have a straight edge to begin cutting fabric strips. Be careful not to move the fabric or you may need to repeat the straightening process.

tip — As you cut through the fabric walk your fingers up the ruler. This allows you to keep pressure on the ruler, making it less likely to slip out of position.

left-handed rotary cutting

Cutting Fabric Strips

Once your fabric has a straight edge you are ready to begin cutting strips.

tip — Place your little finger on the cutting mat and butted up against the ruler when cutting your fabric. This helps to stabilize the ruler and prevent it from sliding on the fabric.

1 Determine the width of the strips needed. The photo above uses 2-1/2"-wide strips. Align the ruler's 2-1/2" marking with the straightened fabric edge. Applying pressure on the ruler with your right hand and beginning at the bottom fold, cut along the left edge of the ruler all the way to the selvages. Walk your fingers up the ruler to hold it securely in place.

2 If your project calls for multiple strips of the same width, use a Post-It® note or masking tape on the ruler as a reminder of the measurement to cut.

Cutting Wider Fabric Strips

tip — It may be necessary to restraighten the fabric after cutting multiple strips.

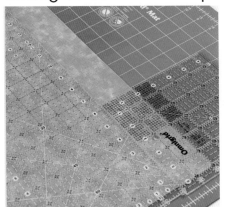

1 To cut wider fabric strips you may need to use two rulers. For example, to cut 8-1/2"-wide strips without access to an 8-1/2"-wide ruler, place a small ruler along the fabric's straight edge measuring in 2". Place the 6-1/2" x 24" ruler against the left edge of the small ruler. Together they total 8-1/2".

2 Cut along the left edge of the rectangular ruler to make an 8-1/2" strip. Walk your fingers up the ruler as you cut to hold it securely in place.

---

left-handed rotary cutting

Subcutting Fabric Strips into Squares

When a project requires multiple squares or rectangles cutting the shapes from strips makes the process go more quickly.

1 To cut squares from the fabric strips, place a folded strip on the cutting mat horizontally in front of you. Square- off the end of the strip and remove the selvages.

2 Determine the size of the squares needed. Align the straightened edge of the strip with the ruler marking that corresponds to the width of the square you wish to cut. Use a Post-It® note on the ruler as a reminder of the size square to cut.

3 Cut the number of squares needed. Use the same process to cut multiple rectangles from fabric strips.

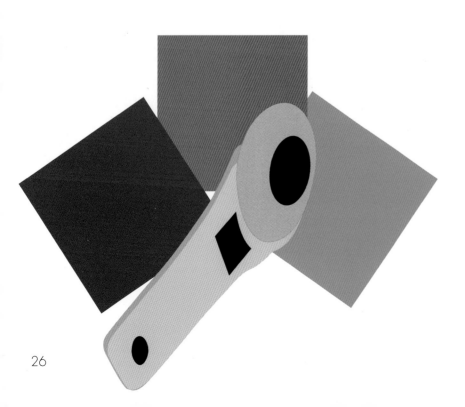

QUILTMAKING BASICS
cutting & piecing half-square triangle blocks

Half-square triangles are used in a variety of block designs. Three techniques are given to make half-square triangle blocks. Choose the one that works best for you. If you need several blocks in the same colorway, follow Technique 3 on page 29.

Technique 1— Making Half-Square Triangle Blocks from Fabric Squares

Add 7/8" seam allowance to the desired finished half-square triangle block size. This is the width to cut your fabric strips. For example, to make a 3" finished half-square triangle block cut the fabric strip 3-7/8" wide; then subcut the strips into 3-7/8" squares. See the chart on page 122 for more size options.

1 To make half-square triangle blocks from fabric squares, place a light fabric strip on the cutting mat horizontally in front of you. Following the instructions in Subcutting Fabric Strips into Squares on page 23, square off the end of the strip and cut as many squares as possible.

2 Cut each square in half diagonally from corner to corner.

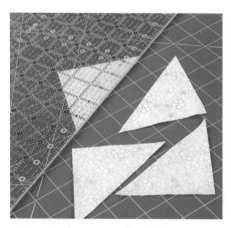

3 Each square will yield two triangles.

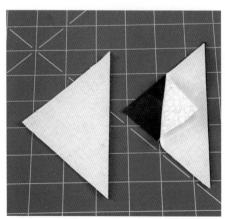

4 Repeat steps 1 - 3 with a dark fabric strip. Layer a light and dark triangle, right sides together.

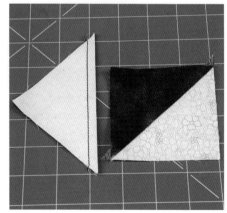

5 Stitch with a 1/4" seam along the long edge of the triangles. Press the seams toward the dark fabric.

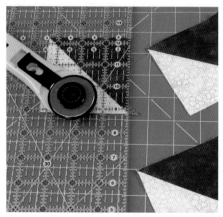

6 Trim the fabric "tails".

Watch a demonstration of this technique at landauerpub.com/videos/halfsquaretriangles.html

cutting & piecing half-square triangle blocks

Technique 2 — Making Half-Square Triangle Blocks from Fabric Strips

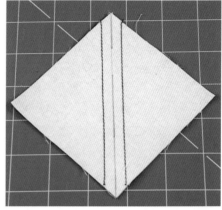

1 To make half-square triangle blocks from fabric strips, place two contrasting strips, right sides together, on the cutting mat horizontally in front of you. Following the instructions in Subcutting Fabric Strips into Squares on page 23, square off the ends of the strips and cut the number of squares needed for your project.

2 Keep the contrasting squares together and draw a diagonal line from corner to corner on the wrong side of one of the squares.

3 Sew a 1/4" seam on either side of the drawn line.

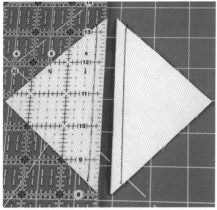

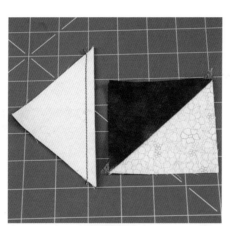

4 Cut on the drawn line and press the seams toward the dark side of the half-square triangles.

5 Trim the fabric "tails".

cutting & piecing half-square triangle blocks

Technique 3 — Making Half-Square Triangle Blocks from Triangles on a Roll™ paper

Triangles on a Roll™ paper allows you to stitch multiple half-square triangle blocks quickly. The paper, which is available in different sizes, is pinned to two rectangles of fabric. The dashed lines on the paper are sewing lines and the solid lines are cutting lines.

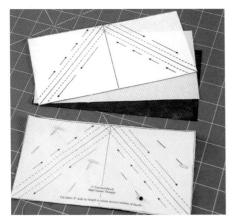

1 Layer two rectangles of contrasting fabric, right sides together, with the lighter fabric on top. Pin the Triangles on a Roll™ paper to the fabrics.

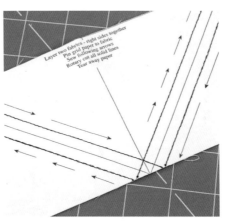

2 Sew on the dashed lines of the paper and remove the pins.

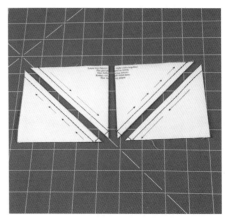

3 Cut on the solid lines of the paper.

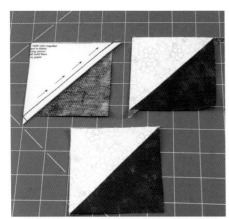

4 Leave the paper on the fabric and press the seams toward the darker fabric. Trim the fabric "tails".

5 Remove the paper, tearing from the center to the outside.

tip — There are other products on the market that allow you to make several half-square triangle blocks at one time. Check with your local quilt shop for information on these products.

QUILTMAKING BASICS
cutting & piecing quarter-square triangle blocks

Quarter-square triangle blocks are used in block and border designs. A single quarter-square triangle block is often referred to as an hourglass block.

Technique 1— Making Quarter-Square Triangle Blocks from Fabric Strips

Add 1-1/4" seam allowance to the desired finished quarter-square triangle block size. This is the width to cut your fabric strips. For example, to make a 3" finished quarter-square triangle block cut the fabric strip 4-1/4" wide; then subcut the squares 4-1/4". See the chart on page 122 for more size options.

1 To make quarter-square triangle blocks from fabric strips, place a light fabric strip on the cutting mat horizontally in front of you. Following the instructions in Subcutting Fabric Strips into Squares on page 23, square off the end of the strip and cut as many squares as possible.

2 Cut each square in half diagonally in both directions. Each square will yield four triangles.

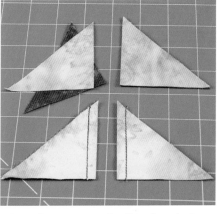

3 Repeat steps 1 - 2 with a dark fabric strip. Layer a light and dark triangle, right sides together, and stitch with a 1/4" seam along a short edge of the triangles.

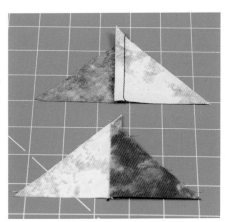

4 Press the seams toward the dark fabric.

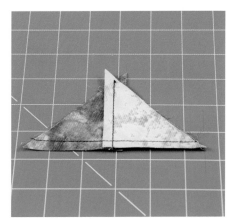

5 Repeat with another pair of triangles. Layer two pairs of triangles, right sides together, with the light fabric on the dark. Check to make sure the seams match. Stitch with a 1/4" seam along the long edge of the pair.

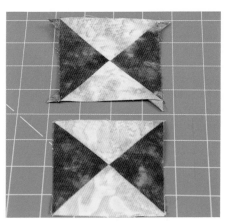

6 Press the pieces open and the seams to one side. Trim the fabric "tails".

Watch a demonstration of this technique at landauerpub.com/videos/quartersquaretriangles.html

cutting & piecing quarter-square triangle blocks

Technique 2— Making Quarter-Square Triangle Blocks from Fabric Squares

1 To make two quarter-square triangle blocks at one time, refer to making half-square triangle blocks on page 27. Make two half-square triangle blocks 1-1/2" larger than needed. Place the blocks right sides together with the light fabric on top of the dark fabric.

2 Draw a diagonal line from corner to corner on the wrong side of the top half-square triangle block.

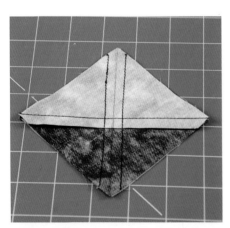

3 Sew a 1/4" seam on either side of the drawn line.

4 Cut on the drawn line. Press the pieces open and the seams to one side.

5 Trim the quarter-square triangle blocks to the size needed for your project. Trim the fabric "tails".

QUILTMAKING BASICS
cutting side- & corner-setting triangles

Quilts with blocks set on the diagonal need setting triangles to complete the design. Use care when cutting side and corner-setting triangles. The straight grain of the fabric should run up and down to prevent distortion when piecing the blocks together. Refer to page 55 for examples of diagonal-set quilt tops.

Side-Setting Triangles

Side-setting triangles are quarter-square triangles with the straight grain of fabric on the long edge of the triangle.

Determine the size of square to cut for side setting triangles by multiplying the finished block size by 1.414 and adding 1-1/4" for the seam allowances.

For example, a 6" finished block x 1.414 = 8.484 + 1.25" = 9-3/4" when rounded up. Refer to the chart on page 123 for other side-setting triangle measurements.

  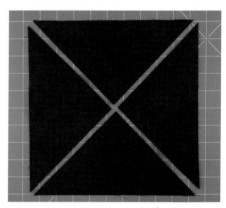

1 Using the formula above or the chart on page 123, determine the size of squares needed to make the side-setting triangles.

2 Cut the square in half diagonally.

3 Cut the square in half diagonally again to make four side-setting triangles.

Corner-Setting Triangles

Corner-setting triangles are half-square triangles with the straight grain of the fabric on the short edge of the triangle.

To determine the size square to cut for corner-setting triangles, divide the finished block size by 1.414 and add .875" for the seam allowances.

For example, a 6" finished block ÷ 1.414 = 4.24 + .875" = 5-1/8" when rounded up. Refer to the chart on page 123 for other corner-setting triangle measurements.

 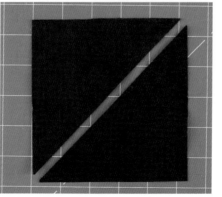

tip — I always cut my setting triangles at least 1/2" larger than required. I trim away the extra fabric after sewing it to my blocks. This may not be necessary, but it gives me peace of mind in case I have miscalculated.

Using the formula above or the chart on page 123, determine the size of squares needed to make the corner-setting triangles. Cut the square in half diagonally to make two corner-setting triangles.

QUILTMAKING BASICS
fussy cutting

Fussy cutting is simply isolating a favorite design or motif in a fabric and cutting around it.

Technique 1 — Fussy Cut a 6-1/2" Square

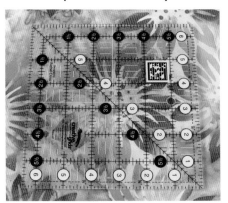  

1 To fussy cut a 6" finished square, lay a 6-1/2" square ruler over the fabric, centering the design under the ruler. The extra 1/2" is the seam allowance.

2 With the ruler held firmly in place, use a rotary cutter to carefully cut around the ruler on all sides.

3 Your design should be centered on your fabric square.

tip — Be certain to add in seam allowances when determining the size of the fussy-cut block.

Technique 2 — Fussy Cut a Larger Square

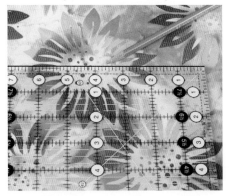 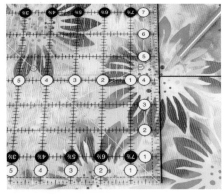 

1 After determining the size of the square needed and choosing a fabric, place a ruler horizontally through the center of the motif you want to highlight. With a marking pencil, draw a line along the edge of the ruler the length of your desired unfinished block size. The example uses an 8-1/2" unfinished block size. The block will finish at 8". The extra 1/2" is seam allowance.

2 In the same way, draw a vertical line through the center of the motif.

3 Divide the unfinished block size in half (8-1/2" ÷ 2 = 4-1/4"). Place the ruler on the drawn center vertical line at this measurement. Draw a vertical line the length of the block along the left outside edge of the ruler. Repeat for the right edge. Connect the outside vertical lines at the corners to complete the square.

4 Using a ruler and rotary cutter, cut out the marked square.

Watch a demonstration of this technique at landauerpub.com/videos/fussycutting.html

fussy cutting

Technique 3
Fussy Cut with a Viewing Window

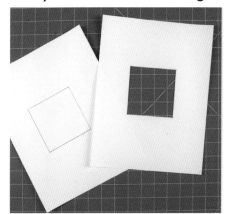

1 Create a viewing window to audition the motif you are fussy cutting using template plastic or a piece of heavy card stock. Draw the size of the square needed on the plastic or card stock and cut the "window" out with scissors or a ruler and craft knife.

2 Place the window over the motif you want to fussy cut and draw around it with a washable marking tool or chalk.

3 Use your ruler to add a 1/4" seam allowance to the square.

tip — Take the viewing window to the quilt shop when choosing fabrics to determine if the motifs will work in the size block you have chosen.

4 Use a ruler and rotary cutter to cut the square.

tip — Mark and cut on the wrong side of the fabric if the motif is visible.

The Four-Patch Quilt on page 90 is made with fussy cut squares.

QUILTMAKING BASICS
chain piecing

Chain piecing is a quick way to stitch several fabric pieces or blocks together at one time. It also saves thread since the pieces are sewn together without stopping and cutting the thread between each piece.

2 Use this method to chain piece the remaining fabric pieces.

1 Sew the first set of fabric pieces together, but do not stop and cut the thread at the end of the piece. Continue to sew a few more stitches and feed the next set of fabric pieces under the presser foot and stitch.

tips —

• Begin your chain piecing by first feeding a piece of folded scrap fabric under the presser foot. This will allow you to easily feed the small fabric squares through the machine without the corners being pulled down into the feed dogs.

• If your sewing machine has a needle down setting, use it while you are chain piecing the fabric pieces together.

3 After all the pieces have been sewn, cut the threads between each piece.

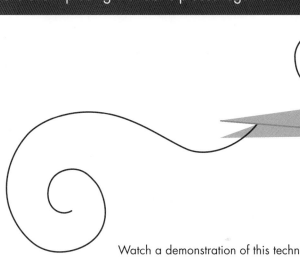

Watch a demonstration of this technique at landauerpub.com/videos/chainpiece.html

QUILTMAKING BASICS
strip piecing

Strip piecing is another time-saving technique that can be used to create many blocks quickly. Strip piecing can be used to join two, four, or as many strips as needed to create your block.

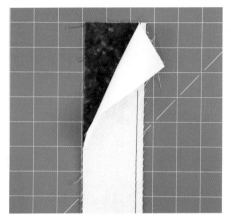

1 Referring to Cutting Fabric Strips on page 22, cut two dark and one light fabric strip. Layer a light and dark fabric strip, right sides together, and stitch along one long edge using a 1/4" seam allowance. Press the strips open with the seam toward the dark strip.

2 Layer the remaining dark strip on the light strip, right sides together, and sew along the long edge. Press the seam toward the dark strip. You are now ready to cut units for nine-patch or rail fence blocks.

tip — Lay strips vertically over the ironing board when pressing. This will keep the strips from becoming distorted as they are pressed.

Sewing Partial Seams

Sewing quilt blocks with partial seams looks complicated but is actually quite simple. Blocks sewn with partial seams consist of a center shape surrounded by four equally sized shapes. Sewing partial seams eliminates the need for set-in seams.

The Bright Hopes block on page 40 is an example of a block sewn with partial seams.

Watch a demonstration of this technique at landauerpub.com/videos/strippiecing.html

QUILTMAKING BASICS
sewing basic blocks

Four-Patch Block

A four-patch block is made up of four equal sized squares in two colors. This block is a good example of how strip piecing is used to make several of the same blocks in less time.

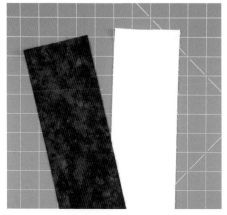

1 Cut a 3-1/2"-wide strip from one light and one dark fabric.

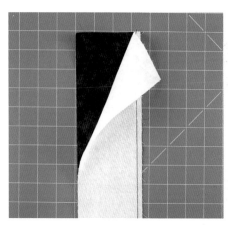

2 Sew the strips, right sides together, using a 1/4" seam allowance. Press the seam toward the darker fabric.

3 Square up the strip set using the same technique shown to straighten the fabric on page 21.

4 Use the ruler to cut 3-1/2"-wide units from the strip set.

5 With right sides together place a light/dark unit on a dark/light unit matching the seams.

6 Sew the units together and press open to make a four-patch block.

The block should measure 6-1/2" and will finish to 6" when sewn into your project.

sewing basic blocks

Nine-Patch Block

A traditional nine-patch block is made up of nine equally sized squares, usually in two contrasting colors. Similar to a four-patch block, the nine-patch block is a good example of how strip piecing is used to make several of the same blocks in less time.

1 Cut three 2-1/2"-wide strips from each of the light and dark fabrics.

2 Sew a light strip to either side of a dark strip using a 1/4" seam allowance. Press the seam allowances toward the dark fabric strip.

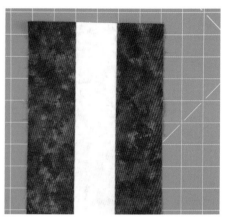

3 Sew the remaining dark strips to either side of the remaining light strip using a 1/4" seam allowance. Press the seam allowances toward the dark fabric strips.

4 Square up the strip sets in the same manner used to straighten the fabric on page 21.

5 Use the ruler to cut 2-1/2" wide units from each of the strip sets.

sewing basic blocks

tip — Nest the units' seam allowances together before sewing.

This means the seam allowance of each unit is going in the opposite direction.

6 With right sides together place a light/dark/light unit on a dark/light/dark unit matching the seams.

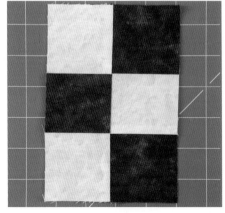

7 Sew the units together and press open.

8 Sew a dark/light/dark unit to the opposite side of the light/dark/light unit and press open to make a nine-patch block.

The block should measure 6-1/2" and will finish to 6" when sewn into your project.

sewing basic blocks

Bright Hopes Block

A Bright Hopes block is sewn with partial seams. The center square of the block is surrounded by four equally sized rectangles.

1 Cut one 2-1/2" fabric square for the center of the bright hopes block.

Cut four 2-1/2" x 4-1/2" fabric rectangles for the outside of the block.

2 Place the center square on top of a rectangle, right sides together. Using a 1/4" seam allowance, join the pieces with a partial seam approximately 2-1/4" long. Press open.

3 Place a rectangle on top of the square/rectangle unit, right sides together. Sew the pieces together. Press open.

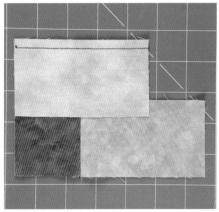

4 Add the third and fourth rectangles in the same manner and press open. Sew the partial seam to finish the Bright Hopes block.

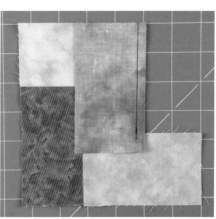

5 The block should measure 6-1/2" and will finish to 6" when sewn into your project.

sewing basic blocks

Pinwheel Block

A pinwheel block is made from four half-square triangle blocks of equal size. When sewn together the half-square triangles should appear to be "blowing" in one direction.

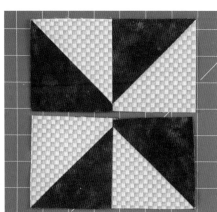

1 Referring to page 27 make four 3-1/2" half-square triangle blocks with contrasting fabrics. Lay the half-square triangles out to form a pinwheel.

2 Using a 1/4" seam allowance, sew the top pair of half-square triangles, right sides together, and press open. Repeat with the bottom pair of half-square triangles.

3 Matching the seam lines, layer the top and bottom units right sides together. Sew the pieces together using a 1/4" seam allowance. Press the block open.

The block should measure 6-1/2" and will finish to 6" when sewn into your project.

The table runner on page 98 is a good example of how to use pinwheel blocks.

Hourglass Block

An hourglass block is another name for a quarter-square triangle block. Refer to page 30 for instructions on how to make an hourglass block.

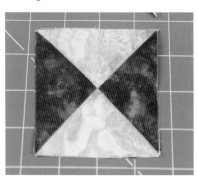

The Hungry Caterpillar Nap Throw on page 110 uses hourglass blocks in a border.

Watch a demonstration of this technique at landauerpub.com/videos/fourpatchpinwheel.html

sewing basic blocks

Rail Fence Block

A rail fence block is traditionally made up of three fabric strips—one each in a light, medium, and dark color. Use the strip piecing method on page 36 to make several blocks quickly.

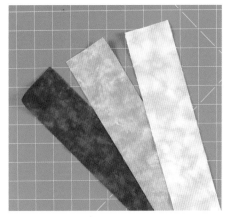

1 Referring to Cutting Fabric Strips on page 22, cut a 2-1/2"-wide light, medium, and dark fabric strip.

2 Layer the light and medium fabric strips, right sides together, and stitch along one long edge with a 1/4" seam allowance. Press the seam toward the medium strip.

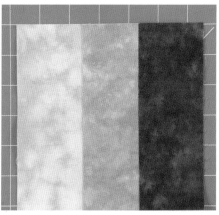

3 Lay the dark strip on the medium strip, right sides together, and sew along the long edge. Press the seam toward the dark strip.

4 Square up the strip sets in the same manner used to straighten the fabric on page 21. Cut the strip set into 6-1/2" segments.

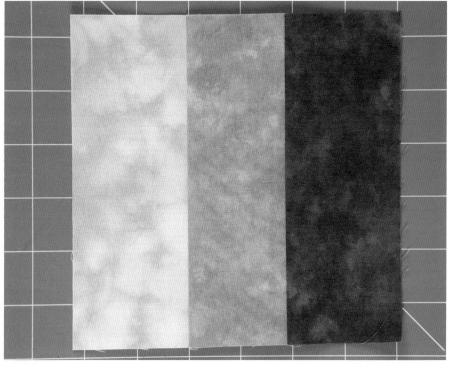

5 The block should measure 6-1/2" and will finish to 6" when sewn into your project.

sewing basic blocks

Flying Geese Block

Flying geese blocks are usually made in multiples and are joined together to be used in other blocks, quilt borders, and sashing.

1 Choose two contrasting fabrics. Cut a 2-1/2" x 4-1/2" rectangle from one fabric and two 2-1/2" squares from the second fabric. Draw a diagonal line, corner to corner, on the wrong side of the squares.

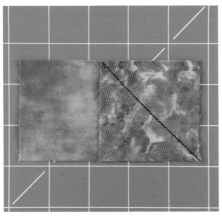

2 Place a square on one side of the rectangle, right sides together. Sew on the drawn line.

3 Place the ruler's 1/4" marking on the sewn line and use a rotary cutter to trim the fabric. Press the pieces open.

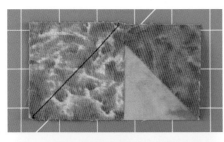

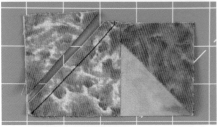

4 Place the second square on the opposite end of the rectangle and repeat steps 2 - 3.

5 The block should measure 2-1/2" x 4-1/2" and will finish 2" x 4" when sewn into your project.

The table topper on page 106 uses flying geese blocks in the sashing and border designs.

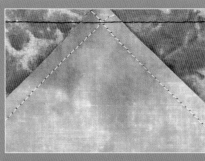

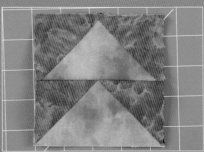

tip — When sewing flying geese blocks together, stitch through the 'X' of the top flying geese block to achieve perfect points.

APPLIQUÉ BASICS

Every quilter has a favorite machine- or hand-appliqué method for creating beautiful quilts. The most commonly used techniques are shown on the following pages. Experiment with adding appliqué to one of your quilting projects.

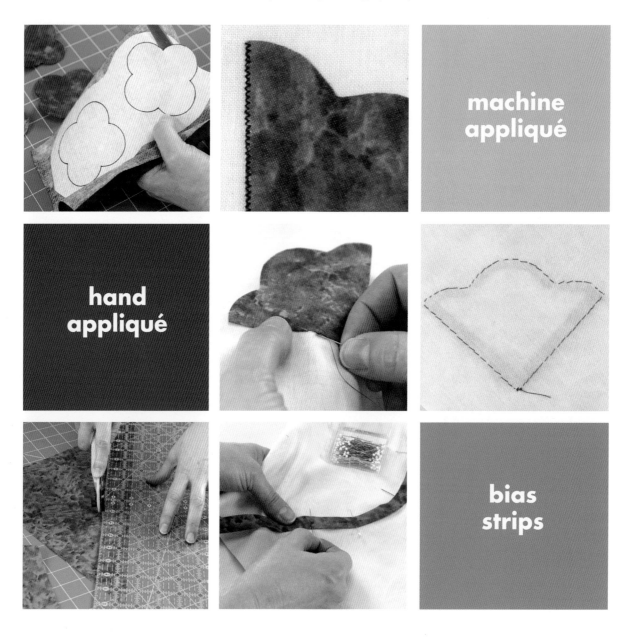

machine appliqué

hand appliqué

bias strips

APPLIQUÉ BASICS
machine appliqué

Using fusible web is the quickest way to prepare shapes for machine appliqué. Before beginning, check to make sure the shapes you are tracing have been reversed. If the shapes have not been reversed, refer to the tip before tracing.

tip — If the appliqué shapes have not been reversed for you, you will need to create a mirror image of the shape. To do this, place the appliqué shapes facedown on a light box or tape them to a sunny window. Trace the appliqué shapes onto a piece of tracing or lightweight paper.

Collect the following supplies before beginning machine appliqué: lightweight fusible web, fine-tip marker or sharp pencil, templates or tracing paper, scissors, open toe or appliqué sewing machine foot, 60/8 sharp sewing machine needle, monofilament thread or thread to match the appliqué, and fabric for appliqués. An appliqué pressing sheet is optional.

1 Place lightweight fusible web, paper-side up, on the reversed appliqué shapes. Trace each shape with a sharp pencil or fine-tip marker.

2 Leave at least 1/4" between shapes that will be cut from the same fabric. If the project has several pieces, mark each shape with a name or number to aid in placement.

3 Cut out the traced shapes from the fusible web leaving 1/8" around each shape. It is not necessary to cut out each individual shape if they are being cut from the same fabric. See the photo with step 5 on page 46.

machine appliqué

4 Larger shapes may be "windowed" by cutting the fusible web from the center of the shape. Cut approximately 1/4" from the traced line. See Tip Box.

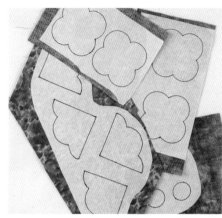

5 Following manufacturer's directions, fuse the appliqué shapes to the wrong side of the fabric. Use a pressing sheet to protect your ironing surface, if desired.

6 Cut out the fused shapes on the traced line. To achieve a smooth cut begin your cut with the back part of the scissor blades.

7 Remove the paper backing and press the shapes in position on the quilt top or background fabric you have chosen.

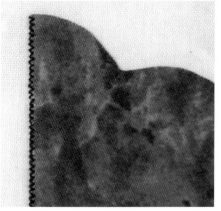

8 Attach an appliqué foot, also referred to as an open toe foot, to your sewing machine. Use a fine zigzag stitch to appliqué the shapes to the quilt top or background fabric. Use a monofilament or a thread color to match or complement your appliqué piece. We used black thread to show the stitching.

tip — To "window" appliqué shapes, cut the fusible web out of the center of the shape. Leave approximately 1/4" of fusible web on either side of the traced shape. Windowing is often done if appliqué shapes are going to be layered. It also reduces stiffness in the finished project.

machine appliqué

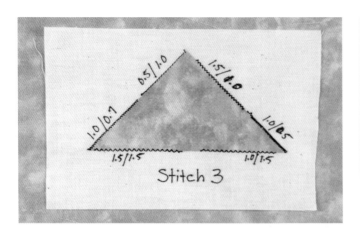

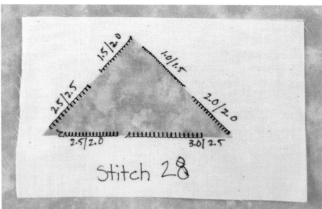

tip — Create an appliqué stitch sampler using the various stitches (zigzag, blanket, etc.) on your machine. Stitch lines in different lengths and widths. Mark each line of stitching with the stitch number, length, and width. Refer to your stitch sampler before beginning each appliqué project.

tip — If you are working on several projects at once, pin a Post-it® note with the stitch number, width, and length to your appliqué project. This will ensure your stitches are consistent when you begin work on your project again.

Freezer paper and a water soluble glue stick are an easy way to prepare appliqué shapes for hand stitching. This technique may also be used for machine appliqué.

Collect the following supplies before beginning hand appliqué: freezer paper, water soluble glue stick, fine-tip marker or sharp pencil, templates or tracing paper, scissors, size 10 between hand needle, monofilament thread or thread to match the appliqué, and fabric for appliqués. An appliqué pressing sheet is optional.

1 Create paper templates by placing freezer paper, matte side up, on the shapes. Trace the shapes with a sharp pencil or fine-tip marker. If the project has several pieces mark each shape with a name or number to aid in placement.

2 Cut out the shapes on the traced line. Cut as smoothly as possible. This will ensure a smooth appliqué shape.

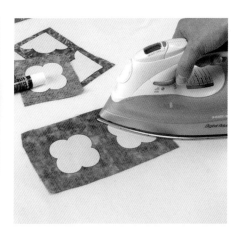

3 Press the freezer paper shape shiny-side down to the **wrong** side of the fabric. Use a few dabs of glue to adhere if necessary.

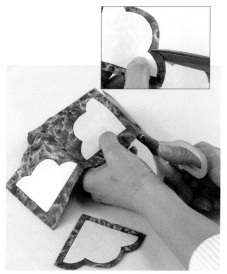

4 Cut the fabric 1/4" away from the shape's outer edge. The 1/4" is the seam allowance. Clip any inside curves or points on the shape within one thread of the freezer paper. This will aid in turning the fabric over the freezer paper. Do not cut into the freezer paper.

hand appliqué

tip — Using a sharp pencil or marking tool, lightly mark a 1/4" guideline around the appliqué shape. This will assist in leaving a 1/4" seam allowance when cutting around the appliqué.

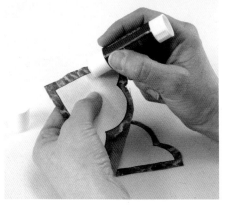

5 Use a water soluble glue stick to apply glue to the seam allowance edge of the appliqué shape.

6 Finger press the fabric edges over the paper edge.

7 After the glue has completely dried, position the shapes on the quilt top or background fabric. Use a dab of glue or spray starch to hold the shapes in place if necessary.

8 Use a size 10 between needle and a small slipstitch to appliqué the shapes in place. Use a monofilament thread or a thread to match the color of the appliqué.

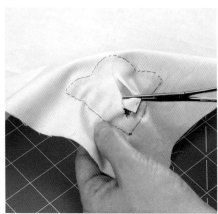

9 The freezer paper must be removed after the pieces have been stitched. From the wrong side, carefully make a slit in the background fabric behind the appliqué pieces. Remove the freezer paper. Trim away the background fabric inside the appliqué shape, leaving a 1/4" seam allowance. Press the appliquéd block from the back and then the front.

APPLIQUÉ BASICS
bias strips

When adding vines or stems to an applilqué project use fabric strips cut on the bias. Fabrics cut on the bias have more stretch and allow you to create curves without puckering.

Fusible Bias Strips

Prepare bias strips in the following manner when using the fusible web method for creating vines and stems for an appliqué project.

1 Before cutting refer to page 21 to straighten the edge of the fabric. To determine the true bias of the fabric, fold the straightened fabric edge over to meet the selvage. The diagonal fold is the true bias.

2 Using a ruler and rotary cutter, cut off the fold.

3 Following manufacturer's instructions press a piece of fusible web to the wrong side of the fabric. The fusible web should be slightly longer and wider than the total size of stems needed.

4 Using a rotary cutter and ruler, cut away the excess fusible web and fabric.

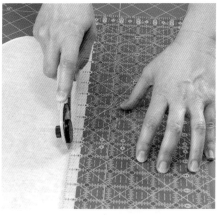

5 Cut strips the width needed for your project. Remove the paper backing and press the strips in position on the quilt top or background fabric you have chosen.

tip — Handle bias strips carefully to avoid stretching them.

triple-fold bias strips

There are several ways to make vines or stems for appliqué projects. The triple-fold bias technique is a quick and easy way to create smooth vines and stems without any raw edges.

1 Determine the true bias of the fabric and cut off the fold following steps 1-2 on page 50.

2 To create a triple-fold bias vine cut the bias strips three times the desired finished vine width. For example, if you want the finished vine to be 1/2"-wide cut the bias strips 1-1/2"-wide.

3 With wrong sides together, fold the strip in thirds and press.

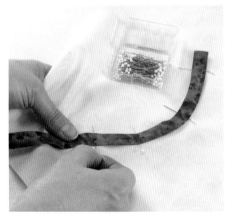

4 Cut vines to the desired length and pin in place on your project. Hand or machine appliqué in place.

tips —

• To create one continuous bias strip, refer to page 78 to learn how to diagonally piece the strips. These continuous strips work well when adding vines or stems to quilt borders.

• If desired, lightly mark the background fabric to indicate the placement of the vine or stem.

Triple-fold Bias Strips
(cut strips three times wider than the desired finished width of the vine or stems)

Desired Finished Size	Cut Strips
3/8"	1-1/8"
1/2"	1-1/2"
5/8"	1-7/8"
3/4"	2-1/4"
1"	3"

ASSEMBLING THE QUILT TOP

There are numerous ways to set blocks in a quilt. Pieced blocks can be framed with sashing strips and cornerstones or alternated with solid blocks. Blocks can also be set on the diagonal to give the quilt a completely different look. Borders frame the quilt top and pull everything together.

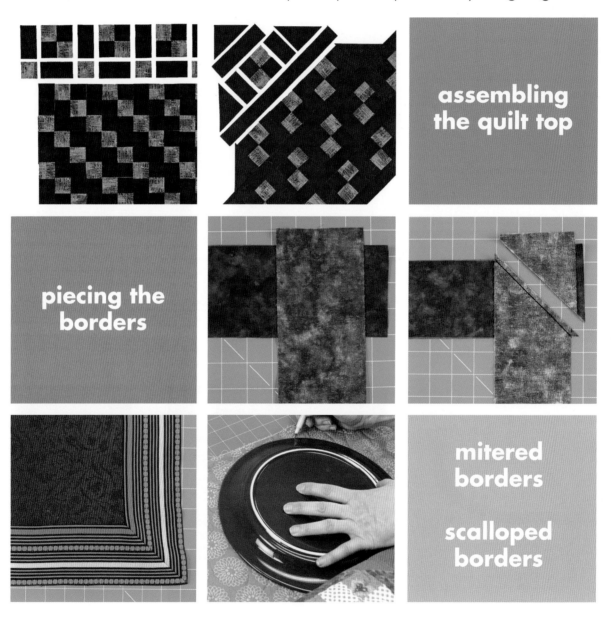

assembling the quilt top

piecing the borders

mitered borders

scalloped borders

ASSEMBLING THE QUILT TOP
straight-set quilt top center

Straight-set quilt top centers can be comprised of pieced blocks, solid squares or alternate blocks, sashing strips, and cornerstones or a combination of any of these units. In a straight-set assembly the units are sewn together in horizontal rows.

Block

Block   Alternate Block

Block-Block Setting

Block-Alternate Block Setting

1 To assemble a straight-set quilt top center, lay the blocks out in horizontal rows on a flat surface. With right sides together, sew the blocks together in each row using a 1/4" seam allowance.

2 Press the seam allowances in each row in one direction. Alternate the seam allowance direction from row to row. For example, press the seam allowances in rows 1, 3, and 5 to the left and press the seam allowances in rows 2, 4, and 6 to the right. This will ensure the seams match when sewing the rows together. See tip on page 39.

3 Join the rows in pairs, right sides together, matching and pinning the blocks' seams.

Sew the joined rows together to complete the quilt top center. Press seam allowances in one direction.

Alternate or Setting Blocks

Alternate blocks, or setting blocks, are placed between the pieced blocks and are usually a solid color.

To determine the size of the setting block, add 1/2" to the finished block size.

For example, a finished 6" block + 1/2" = 6-1/2".

tip — Before assembling the quilt top square-up the blocks to the size listed in the pattern instructions. Squaring-up the blocks means checking to be certain they are all the same size. If you find your blocks are not a consistent size, take the measurement of the smallest one and trim the rest of the blocks to this size. Keep in mind that changing the size of the blocks will also change the dimensions of any alternate blocks, borders, and the finished size of the quilt.

Sashing strips can also be added to the blocks to make them larger. They can then be trimmed to the correct size. Keep in mind that this will change the look of the quilt.

Most importantly, refer to pages 17 - 19 to check and test your 1/4" seam.

straight-set quilt top center

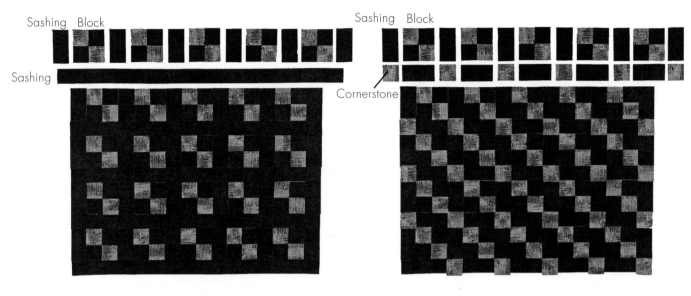

Block-Sashing-Block Setting

Fabric strips sewn between the blocks and rows are referred to as sashing.

Block-Sashing-Cornerstone Setting

Cornerstones are fabric squares sewn to the end of the sashing.

tip — When determining the layout of a quilt top, it helps to see all the pieces placed together before sewing. This gives you the opportunity to move blocks or add another color to enhance the quilt design. A flannel-backed, vinyl tablecloth like those used for outdoor picnic tables and found at discount stores, make great inexpensive design walls. Tack the tablecloth to the wall with the flannel side facing out. Fabric pieces will adhere to the flannel allowing you to play with different quilt layouts and designs.

Quick Fixes For A Quilt Top That Is Too Small

• Add more blocks to each row or add more rows to the quilt top. If you do not have extra pieced blocks, add a solid setting block between each pieced block.

• Add additional borders in a variety of sizes or increase the width of the outer border.

• Add sashing and/or cornerstones to each block.

Diagonal-set quilt top centers are made with blocks set on point at a 45-degree angle. Much like a straight-set quilt top the blocks may be set side-by-side with alternate blocks, sashing or a combination of these units. However, in a diagonal-set quilt, corner- and side-setting triangles are needed to fill in the spaces around the block. The units are then sewn together in diagonal rows.

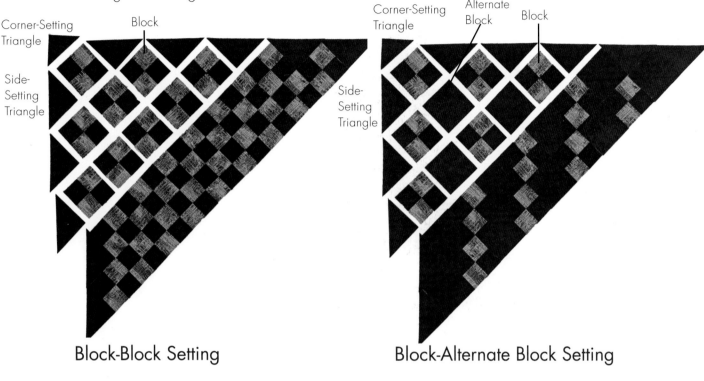

Block-Block Setting

Block-Alternate Block Setting

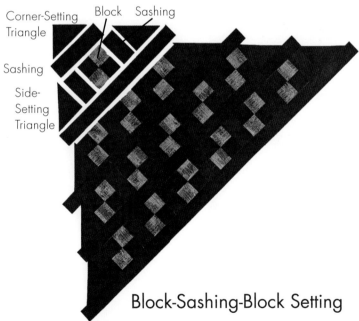

Block-Sashing-Block Setting

tip — I don't pin my small fabric pieces together very often, mainly because it takes too much time and the fabric pieces stay together fairly well on their own. However, when sewing rows together be sure to match the seams and pin. This will ensure the blocks will line up correctly.

ASSEMBLING THE QUILT TOP
straight borders

A border frames the quilt top center and pulls everything together. Single fabric borders or multiple borders made up of blocks or fabric strips are among the most common borders. Repeat colors from the quilt center in the border or choose complementary colors to give the quilt a cohesive look. Borders are also a good place to add some appliqué.

The process for measuring and sewing straight borders to the quilt top center is basically the same no matter what style of straight border is being added. Begin by determining how wide you want the borders. After determining the width of the border strips, follow steps 1 - 3 to cut your border strips to the correct length.

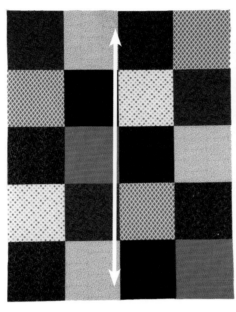 

1 Measure the length of the quilt top through the center. Cut two side border strips to the measured length. Sew the strips to each long side of the quilt top. Press the seam allowances toward the border strips.

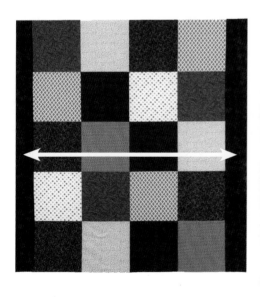 

tip — Math is not my friend; therefore, I will cut my border strips an inch or two longer than the measurement I've taken. After sewing each border strip to the quilt center, I trim the excess fabric length even with the quilt center.

2 Measure the width of the quilt top through the center. Include the side borders in the measurement. Cut two strips to this measurement.

3 Sew the border strips to the top and bottom edges of the quilt top. Press the seam allowances toward the border strips. Repeat steps 1 - 3 to add additional borders to the quilt top.

ASSEMBLING THE QUILT TOP
piecing the borders

Border strips will need to be pieced if the edges of the quilt center are longer than 42". Piecing the border strips on the diagonal makes the seam line less noticeable.

tip — I never cut my border strips before my quilt center is complete and I have measured it myself, even if the pattern I'm following tells me what size to cut my border strips.

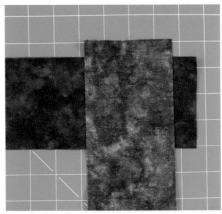

1 Cut strips the width needed for the quilt center border. To join border strips lay one strip right side up on a flat surface. Place a second strip wrong side up and to the right over the first strip.

2 Using a ruler and pencil or other marking tool, draw a diagonal line from corner to corner beginning at the bottom right corner where the strips meet.

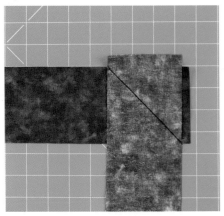

3 Sew on the drawn line.

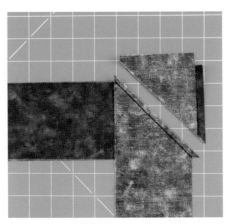

4 Trim 1/4" from the sewn line and press the seam open.

Continue joining the strips until the border strip is the length needed.

tip — If you are using a pieced block border be sure the finished size of the blocks will divide evenly into the quilt center's measurements. You will want all border blocks to fit within the measurements of your quilt center.

ASSEMBLING THE QUILT TOP
mitered borders

Borders can be mitered on any quilt project but they look especially striking when a directional or striped fabric is used in the quilt border. By mitering the corners the borders appear to have a continuous flow around the quilt center. Before cutting the border strips use the formula below to determine the size needed for mitering. Also, keep in mind mitered borders require more fabric. Refer to the tip on this page.

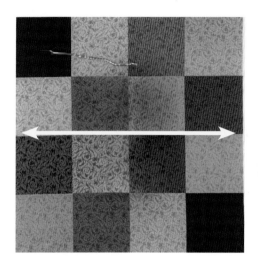
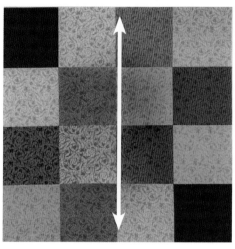

tip —If your quilt top is longer than 42" you will need to piece your mitered borders. Also, you will need to purchase additional fabric if the border fabric you have chosen is a directional print. Extra fabric is needed to match up the designs when diagonally piecing your border strips.

1 Begin by choosing how wide you want the border strips. To calculate the length of the top and bottom border strips, measure the width of the quilt top through the center, side to side. Add the width of the quilt top and the width of two border strips, plus 1/2" seam allowance, plus another 6" for 'just in case'. This measurement equals the size needed for the top and bottom border strips. Cut two strips to this length. See the formula and example below.

2 Determine the length of the side border strips using the same method used for the top and bottom borders. Measure the length of the quilt top through the center, top to bottom. Add the length of the quilt top and the width of two border strips, plus 1/2" seam allowance, plus another 6" for 'just in case'. This measurement equals the size needed for the side border strips. Cut two strips to this length. See the formula and example below.

FORMULA TO DETERMINE THE LENGTH OF MITERED BORDERS:

Top and bottom border strips		Side border strips	
	___" (quilt top width)		___" (quilt top length)
+	___" (width of two border strips)	+	___" (width of two border strips)
+	1/2" (seam allowance)	+	1/2" (seam allowance)
+	6" (just in case)	+	6" (just in case)
=	___" top and bottom border strips	=	___" side border strips

---

EXAMPLE TO DETERMINE THE LENGTH OF MITERED BORDERS FOR A 50" x 72" QUILT TOP

Top and bottom border strips		Side border strips	
	50" (quilt top width)		72" (quilt top length)
+	8" (width of two border strips)	+	8" (width of two border strips)
+	1/2" (seam allowance)	+	1/2" (seam allowance)
+	6" (just in case)	+	6" (just in case)
=	64-1/2" top and bottom border strips	=	86-1/2" side border strips.

mitered borders

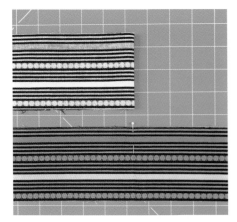

3 Fold each border strip in half lengthwise and lightly press. Open the strip and mark the creased line with a pin.

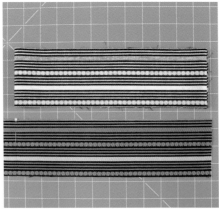

4 Refold the strips in half and in half again. Lightly press. Open the strips and mark the creased lines with a pin.

5 Mark 1/4" on each corner of the quilt center with a water soluble marker, sharp pencil or pin.

6 Fold the quilt center in half, matching the top and bottom raw edges. Lightly press. Open the quilt center and mark the creased line with a pin.

7 Fold the quilt center in half, matching the side raw edges. Lightly press. Open the quilt center and mark the creased line with a pin.

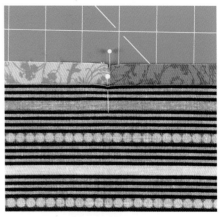

8 Match the pressed marks or pins on the border and the quilt center and pin in place.

mitered borders

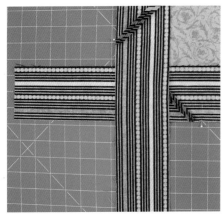

9 The excess fabric will extend past the corner edges.

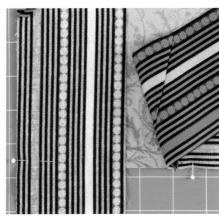

10 Pin a border strip to the quilt top, matching it with the 1/4" marks on the corners of the quilt center.

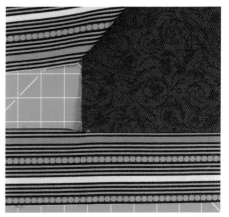

11 Begin sewing at the 1/4" corner mark, backstitching a couple of stitches to secure. Continue sewing the border to the quilt center, stopping at the opposite 1/4" mark and backstitching. Press the seam allowance toward the border.

Repeat to attach the remaining borders to the quilt center.

12 To miter the corners, lay the quilt center, right side up, on an ironing board or flat, iron-safe surface. Lay one border on the surface with the adjoining border laying over it.

13 Fold the top border at a 45-degree angle. Press.

14 Fold the quilt center diagonally with right sides together. The borders should now be laying right sides together with the creased border on top.

mitered borders

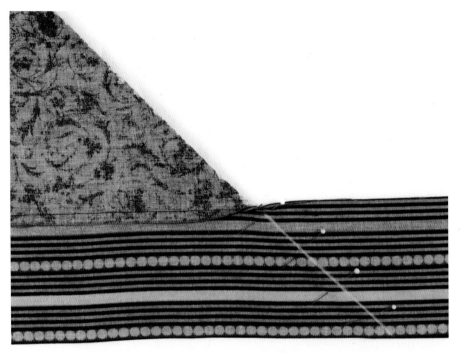

16 Beginning at the quilt center's inside corner and backstitching a couple of stitches, sew on the pressed line. Check the mitered corner from the right side to be certain there are no gaps in your stitching and the corner lies flat.

15 Mark the pressed line with a sharp pencil or marking tool. Pin the borders together along the pressed line.

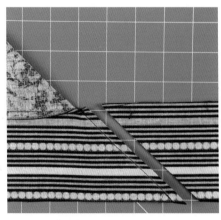

17 Trim the seam to 1/4" and press seams open.

18 Pressing the seams open will help the corner lie flat.

Repeat to miter the other three corners.

tip — If you are planning to add more than one mitered border, join all of the border strips together lengthwise first. Sew to the quilt center as one unit. This will make it easier to miter the corners.

ASSEMBLING THE QUILT TOP
scalloped borders

Adding a gently curving scalloped border to a quilt center softens the look of the finished quilt. Scallops are cut after the quilting has been completed.

After the quilting has been completed, measure the width and length of the quilt top. Choose the width of the scallops, keeping in mind the width will need to divide evenly into the measurements of the quilt top.

1 Using a chalk or water soluble marker, mark the quilt top with a dot the width of your scallop. The example above shows an 8" scallop.

2 Connect the dots by drawing a line between them. This line represents the top of each scallop.

3 Decide how deep or shallow you want the scallops to be and place a dot at this measurement under the first dots. The example above shows 1-1/2" deep scallops.

FORMULA TO DETERMINE THE NUMBER OF SCALLOPS ON QUILT TOP:

Top and bottom scallops   *Side scallops*

	___"	(quilt top width)		___"	(quilt top length)
÷	___"	(width of scallops)	÷	___"	(width of scallops)
=	___	top and bottom scallops	=	___	side scallops

EXAMPLE TO DETERMINE NUMBER OF 8" SCALLOPS ON A 64" x 88" QUILT TOP

	64"	(quilt top width)		88"	(quilt top length)
÷	8"	(scallops)	÷	8"	(scallops)
=	8	scallops on top/bottom borders	=	11	scallops on side borders

---

EXAMPLE TO DETERMINE NUMBER OF 12" SCALLOPS ON AN 84" x 96" QUILT TOP

	84"	(quilt top width)		96"	(quilt top length)
÷	12"	(scallops)	÷	12"	(scallops)
=	7	scallops on top/bottom borders	=	8	scallops on side borders

scalloped borders

5 Refer to Bias Binding on page 80 to create binding strips for the quilt. The bias binding will be sewn to the drawn scallop lines on the quilt. The excess batting and backing will be trimmed away after the binding is attached and before it is turned to the back of the quilt.

4 Connect the bottom set of dots following the curve of a rounded lid, plate, or glass. Be sure the top of the curve hits the top line between the top set of dots. Join the scallops at the end of each border to create a curve at each corner of the quilt top.

Note: We darkened the marking line for illustration purposes.

tip — If you choose to create deep scallops with a sharp adjoining point or "V" the quilt top may be more difficult to bind.

tip — Before marking your quilt top you may want to make a pattern or template to insure the scallops will fit properly on the quilt top. Use large sheets of paper or cut a piece of freezer paper 3" x the width and length of the quilt top. Rolls of freezer paper can be found at the grocery store.

tip — When cutting bias strips for a project with scalloped edges, cut 1 - 2 extra strips. The scalloped edges take a bit more binding.

Single Straight Borders

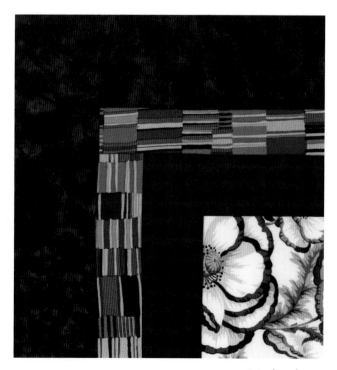

Multiple Straight Borders

border examples

Pieced Block Borders

Mitered Border   Scalloped Border

FINISHING THE QUILT

Layering, quilting, and adding binding are a few of the final steps in the quilt making process. These last steps are just as important as the beginning ones.

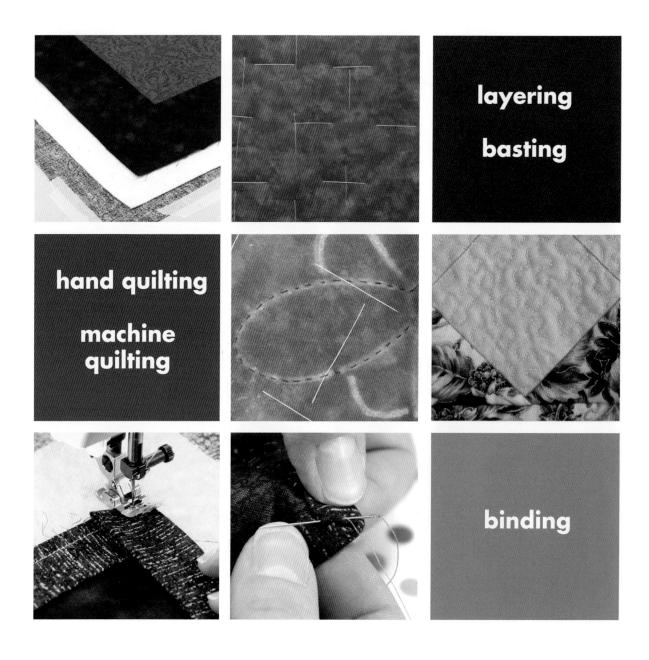

layering

basting

hand quilting

machine quilting

binding

FINISHING THE QUILT
batting and backing fabric

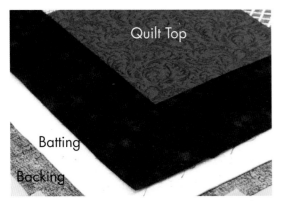

Quilt Top

Batting

Backing

Batting

Batting is the layer between the quilt top and backing and is available in different lofts or thicknesses. When choosing the batting consider how the quilt will be used. For example, if the quilt will be displayed on a wall use a thinner, low-loft batting. This will allow the quilt to hang flat.

Always read the manufacturer's instructions before purchasing batting. You will find recommendations for distance between stitches for hand and machine quilting on the label, as well as other information.

The batting should be large enough to extend beyond each side of the quilt top.

tip — Unroll the batting a few days before you are going to need it. This will help release any creases so it will lay flatter between the quilt top and backing fabric. It will also restore the batting's loft.

Backing Fabric

The fabric chosen for the quilt back should be the same quality material and complement the front of the quilt. Unless you are making a smaller quilt—36" square or less—you will need to piece the backing fabric.

The examples below show how to piece backing for larger quilts.

The quilt back should be at least 4" wider than the quilt top on each side. Trim the selvages before cutting and sewing the backing segments.

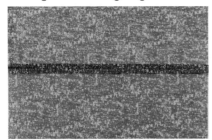

40" to 60" pieced backing

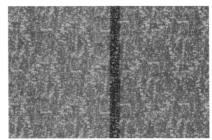

61" to 80" pieced backing

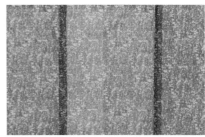

81" to 120" pieced backing

FORMULA TO DETERMINE THE AMOUNT OF BACKING FABRIC NEEDED:	
	___" (quilt top length)
+	4" (for extra backing)
÷	36"
=	___ yards
×	2*
=	___ yards backing fabric
(round up to nearest 1/4 yard)	

*If your quilt width is 36" or less, multiply x1
 If your quilt width is 80" or more, multiply x 3

EXAMPLE TO DETERMINE THE AMOUNT OF BACKING FABRIC NEEDED FOR A 60" x 78" QUILT TOP:	
	78" (quilt top length)
+	4" (for extra backing)
÷	36"
=	2.27 yards
×	2
=	4.75 yards backing fabric
(rounded up 1/4 yard)	

tip — I always purchase an extra 1/2 yard of backing fabric, just in case I have miscalculated my measurements. Plus, I like to sew my backing segments together with a 1/2" seam allowance instead of the usual 1/4".

FINISHING THE QUILT
layering the backing, batting, and quilt top

The three layers of a quilt—the backing, batting, and quilt top—are referred to as a quilt sandwich. A flat surface large enough to accommodate the size of the quilt backing when sandwiching the quilt pieces is needed.

tip — If you are planning to use a quilting design that needs to be marked on your quilt top, do not layer the backing, batting, and quilt top yet. Mark the design on your quilt top before layering the pieces together. Refer to page 70 for marking designs on the quilt top.

1 Begin by laying the pressed backing fabric on a flat surface. The right side of the backing fabric is facing down; the wrong side is facing up. Smooth out any wrinkles in the fabric, working from the center out to the edges. Do not stretch the fabric. Use pieces of masking tape to secure the backing fabric to the flat surface. Continue to smooth out the backing fabric as you place the tape around its edges.

2 Center the batting on top of the backing fabric. Smooth it out beginning at the center and working out to the edges. The batting should be an inch or so smaller than the backing fabric.

tip — If you decide to hire someone to quilt your quilt, talk to other quilters or check with your local quilt shop for information on quilters for hire in your area. I do recommend trying your hand at quilting at least one of your projects. You may surprise yourself.

3 Place the quilt top, right side up, on the batting. Center and smooth it out as you did for the backing fabric and batting. The quilt top should not extend over the batting and backing fabric. These three layers are the quilt sandwich.

FINISHING THE QUILT
basting the quilt sandwich

Basting the quilt sandwich will hold the three layers together while hand or machine quilting. This can be accomplished with small (1"-1-1/2") nickel-plated, rust-proof safety pins or a needle and thread.

1 Open the safety pins and scatter them across the quilt surface.

2 Beginning at the quilt center, insert a safety pin through all three layers of the quilt sandwich. Place a Kwik Klip™ at the point where the tip of the safety pin will come up through the layers. Close the safety pin using the Kwik Klip™.

tip — A grapefruit spoon may be used in place of a Kwik Klip™. You can also use both hands to pin baste the quilt sandwich, but be careful not to 'bunch up' the layers of the quilt sandwich while trying to close the safety pins. This could cause puckers in the backing fabric.

tip — It will help to know what type of quilting design you plan to use on the quilt. You will not want to place safety pins in those areas. For example, if you will be stitching-in-the-ditch (page 75), do not place safety pins in or near the seams to be quilted.

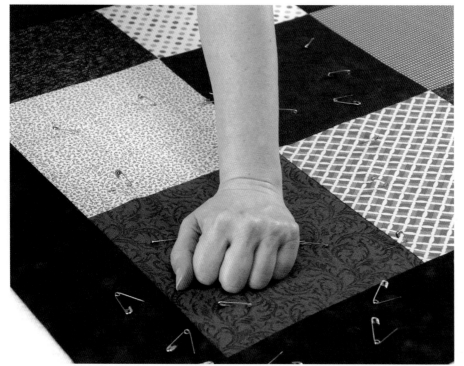

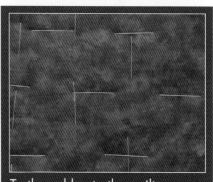

3 Continue to place safety pins across the quilt's surface working from the center out in a random pattern. Smooth the quilt top as the pins are added to remove any wrinkles that may have been created while pinning. Safety pins should be placed approximately four-inches apart. Check by placing your fist anywhere on the quilt top. Your fist should be close to or touching a safety pin on all sides. Repeat this test in several areas of the quilt top.

To thread baste the quilt sandwich, use a cotton thread and long needle for going through all three layers. Make stitches approximately 2" long and 3" – 4" apart in a vertical and horizontal grid across the quilt surface. Use a thimble to help push the needle through the layers.

Marking the Quilt Top with Stencils

It is easier to mark the quilt top for quilting before layering it with the backing fabric and batting. If you missed the tip in Layering the Backing, Batting, and Quilt Top on page 68, don't worry; you can still mark the design with the safety pins in place. You just may need to remove a few pins as you go.

1 Using masking tape, secure the quilt top to a flat surface. Place the stencil over the area to be quilted and mark with your chosen marking tool.

Repeat this process until the quilt top is marked as desired.

2 Connect the stencil's open or interrupted lines. Baste the quilt following Basting the Quilt Sandwich directions on page 69.

Note: If you have pin basted your quilt sandwich, use the steps given, but remove or flip the safety pins to the side if they interfere with the stencil markings.

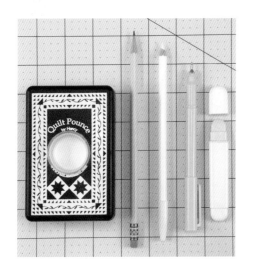

tip — There are a wide variety of marking products available and each has different instructions. Carefully read the manufacturer's instructions before choosing a marking tool. Some markings may become permanent if the instructions are not followed. Don't take a chance and ruin a quilt you have worked many hours to create.

quilting the quilt

Marking the Quilt Top with Tape

Use masking tape or painter's tape to mark your quilt top for straight-line or grid quilting. The tapes are available in different widths and provide a quick way to mark a quilt top. It can be placed before or after the quilt layers are basted together.

tips — Don't leave the tape on your quilt for a long period of time as it may leave a sticky residue.

If you accidentally sew over the tape, keep going and remove the tape as usual. Use a tweezers to pick the tape out from under any stitches.

1   Place strips of tape in one direction on the quilt top. Sew close to the edges of the tape. Do not stitch over it or any safety pins.

tip — If you don't have a large enough surface to lay out the quilt sandwich, check with your local quilt shop, library, or church to see if they will let you push a few tables together to prepare your quilt for quilting. A clean floor also works well.

2   Remove the strips of tape and reposition them on the quilt top in the opposite direction. Sew next to the tape edges. Remove the tape.

All quilts can be hand or machine quilted. Hand quilting showcases small, even stitches. If you choose to hand quilt, use the needle and thread technique on page 69 to baste the quilt sandwich. Keep in mind hand quilting can be time consuming.

Choosing to Hand or Machine Quilt

You may wish to hand quilt your quilt when:
- time is not an issue
- appliqués or designs on the quilt top are intricate
- the quilt top is hand pieced
- the quilt will not be heavily used
- you are mimicking the look of an antique quilt
- the stitches will be an integral part of the quilt

You may wish to machine quilt your quilt when:
- the quilt top is machine pieced
- you want to finish the project more quickly
- the quilt will be used and laundered often

tip — Begin any type of quilting in the center of the quilt top and work out to the edges. This will help prevent any bunching or puckering that might occur.

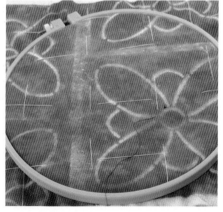 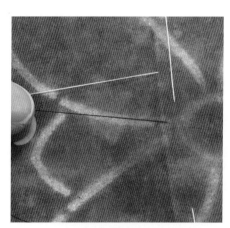 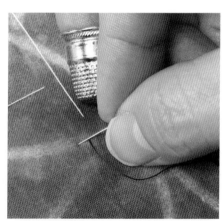

1 Place the basted quilt sandwich in a hoop or frame and tighten. Thread a size 10 between needle with an 18" length of 100 percent cotton quilting thread. Knot the end of the thread. Insert the needle into the top and batting of the quilt sandwich a few inches from where you will start quilting. Do not go through the backing fabric. Bring the needle to the surface on the line where you want to make the first stitch. Tug lightly on the thread until the knot goes through the quilt top and is embedded in the batting.

2 To make a running stitch, hold the needle between your thumb and index finger. A thimble on your middle finger will help push the needle through the quilt layers. Put your other hand under the hoop to guide the needle where you want the stitches to go.

hand quilting

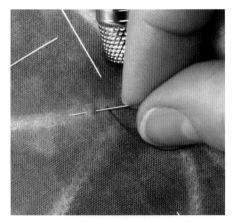

3 Push the needle through the layers of the quilt. As you feel the tip of the needle come through the back of the quilt move the finger under the quilt pushing the needle forward and up to the surface of the quilt. Pull the thread through and begin another stitch.

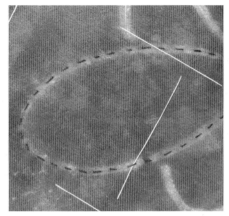

4 It is important to try to keep the stitches uniform in size.

As you practice and feel more comfortable you can take more than one stitch at a time on your needle.

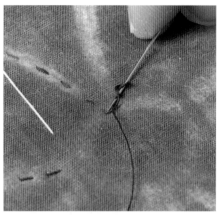

5 To end your stitching, wrap the thread around the needle approximately three times and close to the quilt top.

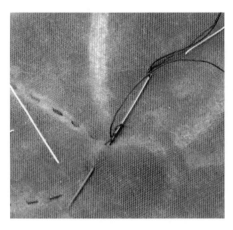

6 Insert the needle into the ending stitch, going through the quilt top and batting only. Bring the needle back up to the surface approximately 1/2" away from the stitching.

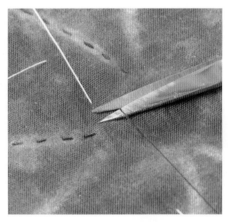

7 Bury the knot in the batting in the same manner you did to begin quilting. Clip the thread close to the quilt surface.

tip — When wrapping the thread around the needle to make a knot, use a slight amount of tension when holding the tail of the thread. This will help keep the thread wrap together.

FINISHING THE QUILT
machine quilting

Enhance your quilt top by using any of the machine quilting options given. The different styles of machine quilting can also be combined on the quilt top. Attach a walking or even-feed foot to the sewing machine before beginning. The walking foot moves the layers of the quilt through the sewing machine evenly.

Bringing up the bobbin thread

1 Bring the bobbin thread to the top of the quilt sandwich before beginning any of the quilting options shown. Place the quilt sandwich under the presser foot where you want to begin quilting. Hold the top thread in your left hand and lower the needle into the quilt sandwich.

2 Lower the presser foot and take a stitch. The bobbin thread should appear on the quilt top.

tip — If your sewing machine has a needle down feature, engage it while doing any type of machine quilting.

3 Hold the top and bobbin threads while sewing the first few stitches. This will secure the beginning stitches.

tip — If you decide to hire someone to quilt your quilt, talk to other quilters or check with your local quilt shop for information on quilters for hire in your area. I do recommend trying your hand at quilting at least one of your projects. You may surprise yourself.

machine quilting

Stitching-in-the-Ditch

In-the-ditch quilting refers to quilting just inside the seam line. Stitching-in-the-ditch around a pieced block makes it stand out from the quilt background. This stitching method is also used to stabilize the quilt before adding other quilting designs and keeps the quilt layers from shifting. It is one of the easiest machine quilting techniques to master.

1   Bring up the bobbin thread (page 74) and stitch-in-the-ditch along the seam lines that join the rows of blocks in your quilt. This will stabilize the quilt top if you are adding other quilting designs.

Pull the seam apart while stitching by placing your hands on the fabric on either side of the needle. Choose monofilament or a thread color that will disappear into the seam lines.

Note: We used black thread so the stitches would show more clearly.

2   Stitch into the seam line or as close as possible. Stitch to the end of the seam and secure the thread with two small backstitches. Repeat to stabilize other seam lines in the quilt.

Stitch-in-the-Ditch Quilting

Use steps 1 - 2 above to stitch-in-the-ditch in the seam lines of pieced blocks in a quilt.

In-the-ditch quilting was used to quilt the table topper on page 90.

machine quilting

Free-Motion Machine Quilting

Free-motion quilting takes practice, but offers many more options when quilting your quilt. Drop the feed dogs and attach a darning or free-motion foot to the sewing machine before beginning. Continue to use the needle down feature on the machine. You control the stitch length and speed of the machine with your hands and the pressure applied to the foot pedal.

Stipple or Meander Quilting

Stipple or meander quilting resembles puzzle pieces and can be used as an all-over pattern on a quilt top. It can be used around appliqué shapes to add texture.

Echo Quilting

Echo quilting is stitching around the shape of a motif or design, repeating it multiple times. The space between the quilting lines should be between 1/4" - 1/2" apart.

Outline Quilting

Outline quilting is sewing a 1/4" away from a seam line or the edge of an appliqué shape.

tip — Always practice the stitches you are going to use before trying them out on a 'real' quilt top. Layer scraps of leftover fabric and batting to create a small quilt sandwich. Pin baste with a few safety pins and practice until you achieve a steady rhythm and stitch length.

tip — Check with your local quilt shop for classes on free-motion quilting.

FINISHING THE QUILT
tying the quilt

Tying a quilt is a great alternative if you are uncomfortable hand or machine quilting your first quilt. Use yarn or perle cotton and a size 14 to 18 darning needle. The larger eye on the needle will accommodate a heavier thread or yarn.

The quilt layers should be pin-basted before tying. This will ensure the layers won't slip as the needle is being pushed through and pulled back up to the top of the quilt. It is also a good idea to stitch-in-the-ditch of the quilt's seam lines in case the fabric stretches while tying.

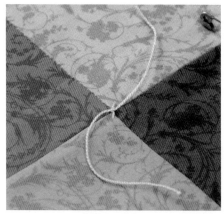

1 Thread the darning needle with an 18" single strand of perle cotton thread or yarn. Start at the center of the quilt top and make a single running stitch approximately 1/8" to 1/4" long through all the quilt layers beginning and ending on the quilt top. Leave a 3" thread tail. Cut the thread on the needle side leaving a 3" tail.

2 Tie a square knot on the quilt top with the thread ends. Pull the knot tight to secure it, but do not pull it so tight that it causes puckers on your quilt top.

3 Continue tying the rest of the quilt in the same manner. Clip all the thread ends to the same length.

tips —
• Tie the quilt approximately every 4" to keep all three layers secure.

• To tie a square knot, place the thread ends right over left and then left over right.

You may also use a longer piece of thread or yarn and take running stitches at regular intervals without cutting the thread. Continue taking stitches until coming to the end of the thread. Cut the yarn at equal intervals between each stitch and then knot.

FINISHING THE QUILT
binding the quilt

Now that the quilt has been quilted it is time to cover the raw edges with binding. Binding is made with strips of fabric that are pieced together, usually on the diagonal.

French-fold, Continuous Binding

The most common type of binding is French-fold, or double-fold, binding. It is a favorite among quilters since the double layer of fabric protects the edges of the quilt and makes it more durable.

I generally cut my binding strips 2-1/2" wide for a 1/2" finished binding. Other binding size options are below.

To calculate the number of binding strips needed for your quilt add the four outside measurements of the quilt plus 12". Divide that number by 40" (usable fabric) to determine how many binding strips are needed.

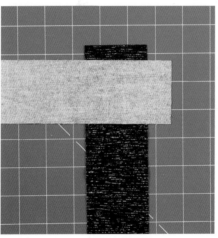

1 To make one continuous binding strip, lay one strip, right side up on a flat surface. Place a second strip, wrong side up, perpendicular and to the left, over the first strip.

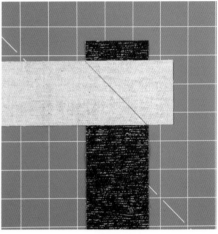

2 Using a ruler and sharp pencil or marking tool, draw a diagonal line from corner to corner beginning at the bottom right corner where the strips meet.

FRENCH-FOLD BINDING STRIPS
(cut strips four times wider than the desired finished binding width and add 1/2" for seam allowances)

Desired Finished Size	Cut Strips
1/4"	1-1/2"
3/8"	2"
1/2"	2-1/2"
5/8"	3"
3/4"	3-1/2"
7/8"	4"

FORMULA TO DETERMINE THE NUMBER OF BINDING STRIPS NEEDED:

	___"	(top, bottom & side measurements of quilt)
+	12"	(just in case)
÷	40"	(usable fabric)
=	___	(number of binding strips needed; round up if needed)

EXAMPLE TO DETERMINE THE NUMBER OF BINDING STRIPS NEEDED FOR A 56" X 78" QUILT TOP:

	268"	(top, bottom & side measurements of quilt)
		56 (top) + 56 (bottom) + 78 (side) + 78 (side)
+	12"	(just in case)
÷	40"	(usable fabric)
=	7	(number of binding strips needed; round up if needed)

binding the quilt

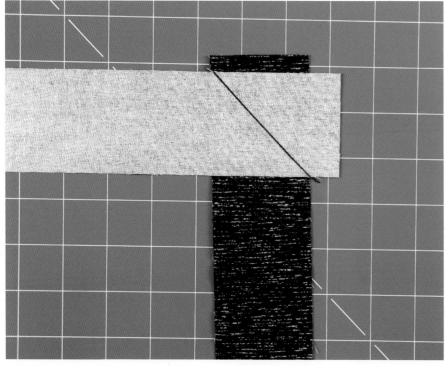

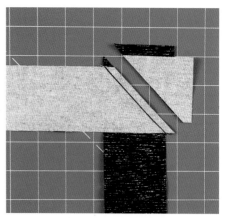

4 Trim 1/4" from the sewn line.

3 Sew on the drawn line.

5 Press the seam open. Repeat until all the binding strips have been joined into one continuous piece.

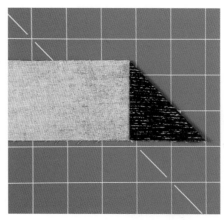

6 Fold one end of the binding strip at a 45-degree angle and press.

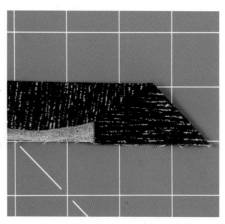

7 Fold the binding strip in half along the long edge and press.

tip — Before attaching the binding to your quilt, you may want to add a hanging sleeve. Refer to Adding a Sleeve before Binding on page 85.

binding the quilt

Bias Binding

Fabric strips cut on the bias grain can be used to bind quilts with scalloped or curved edges. Strips cut on the bias have more stretch allowing them to go around curves smoothly. Bias cut strips also help the binding on a scalloped quilt lie flat. Referring to Straightening the Fabric on page 21, straighten the edge of the binding fabric.

1 To determine the true bias of the fabric, fold the straightened fabric edge over to meet the selvage.

2 The diagonal fold is the true bias. Using a ruler and rotary cutter, cut off the fold.

3 Cut the number of bias strips the width needed for your project.

Handle the strips carefully to avoid stretching them. Join the strips together into one continuous strip by following the instructions in French-fold, Continuous Binding on page 78.

FINISHING THE QUILT
attaching binding to the quilt top

Trim the batting and quilt backing so it extends approximately 2-1/2" beyond the quilt top edge. You will trim this excess batting and backing before turning the binding to the back of the quilt.

tip — Keep any leftover binding pieces from your projects together. Sew them together when a scrappy binding is needed on a quilt.

The quilt on page 94 is an example of a scrappy binding.

1 Use a ruler to mark 1/4" inside both edges of the four corners of the quilt top. These marks indicate where to stop sewing so you can miter the corners of the binding strip.

2 Pin the beginning end of the binding strip (the end with the 45-degree angle) to the right side of the quilt top. Start the strip in the center of the bottom or side edge of the quilt top. Align the raw edge of the binding strip with the raw edge of the quilt top.

3 Set the needle-down function on your machine and begin sewing with a 1/4" seam allowance approximately 2" from the angled edge.

4 Stop sewing when you reach the 1/4" mark at the corner of the quilt top. Backstitch a few stitches and remove the quilt from beneath the presser foot. Cut the threads.

5 Fold the binding strip up to create a 45-degree angle. The raw edge of the binding strip should remain aligned with the raw edge of the quilt top. Press with your fingers to create a slight crease in the binding strip.

attaching binding to the quilt top

6 Hold the diagonal fold in place with one finger and bring the binding strip down to line up with the raw edge of the quilt top. Secure with a pin if desired.

7 Place the quilt with the mitered binding corner under the presser foot and begin sewing at the top of the horizontal fold. Secure the first few stitches by backstitching. Continue sewing the binding to the quilt top, mitering each corner in the same way.

8 When you have reached the beginning point, tuck the end of the binding strip inside the folded end. Trim the end of the binding strip as needed to place inside the folded edge.

9 Continue sewing to the starting stitches. Backstitch a few stitches to secure.

10 Use a long acrylic ruler and rotary cutter to remove the excess batting and backing from the quilt. Carefully cut away the extra batting and backing on all sides. You are now ready to turn the binding to the back of the quilt top.

tip — I do not pin the entire binding to my quilt top before stitching it. It just takes too much time. I pin the first 6" or so of the binding to the quilt top and then begin sewing. Check regularly to make sure the raw edges of the binding are aligned with the raw edges of the quilt top as it is fed through the machine.

attaching binding to the quilt top

Two additional techniques for joining the binding ends are shown below. Experiment to find your favorite method for joining the binding ends.

Technique 1

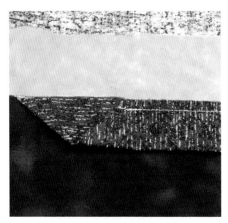

1 Prepare the continuous binding strip with the starting end folded at a 45-degree angle. Align the raw edge of the binding strip with the raw edge of the quilt top. Begin stitching at the beginning of the 45-degree fold. Continue sewing the binding, mitering the corners.

2 When you have reached the beginning point and the needle is at the top of the diagonal fold, stop sewing with the needle down in the fabric.
Lay the extra binding over the diagonal fold and make a straight cut to remove the excess binding where the two meet.

3 Place the binding tail inside the diagonal fold and continue sewing over the beginning stitches.

Technique 2

1 Prepare the continuous binding strip and align the raw edge of the binding strip with the raw edge of the quilt top. Start stitching approximately 5" from the beginning of the binding strip. Continue sewing the binding, mitering the corners. When you are 10" - 15" from the beginning point, stop sewing and remove the quilt from under the presser foot.

2 Lay the 10" ending binding strip over the 5" beginning binding strip. Fold and crease the ending binding strip where it meets the beginning strip. Measure and mark a 1/4" from the crease. Cut the ending binding strip at the mark. With right sides facing, join the binding ends by stitching with 1/4" seam. Check to make sure the binding strip is not twisted and will lie flat on the quilt top. Press the seam open.

Fold the binding strip in half lengthwise and continue sewing.

Backstitch to secure the binding after reaching the starting stitches.

After the binding has been sewn to the quilt front, it needs to be turned to the back and stitched in place.

tip — It is not necessary to place clips on the entire quilt. Move the clips around the quilt's edges as needed. I also use a clip to mark where I began turning the binding to the back of the quilt top.

1 Metal hairclips or binding clips will help keep the binding in place while it is being sewn to the quilt back. Turn the binding to the back of the quilt, covering or aligning the binding stitch line with the folded edge of the binding. Place clips at 4" - 5" intervals.

2 Using a slipstitch, hand-stitch the folded edge of the binding to the back of the quilt. Stitches should be 1/4" - 3/8" apart.

Check frequently to be sure the stitches are not showing on the quilt top.

3 As you come to each corner, fold a miter in it and take a couple of stitches in each fold to secure it.

Slipstitch

A slipstitch is used to attach the binding to the quilt top.

- Thread the needle with a single strand of thread in a color that will blend in with the binding. Knot the end.
- Insert the needle into the quilt backing, a few stitches above the binding's fold. Bring the point of the needle out at the edge of the binding's fold. Keep the stitch short.
- Pull the needle through and insert it just behind the space the thread came out in the first stitch.
- Run the needle inside the fold for a short stitch, bringing it out along the folded edge again.
- Repeat the stitch until the binding is attached to the quilt top.

FINISHING THE QUILT
adding a hanging sleeve

A hanging sleeve is a good idea if the quilt will be displayed on a wall. A dowel or flat board placed through the opening of the hanging sleeve lets the quilt hang flat. Using the same fabric for the hanging sleeve and backing fabric will make the sleeve less noticeable if you decide to use the quilt on a bed instead of a wall. The hanging sleeve can be added before or after the binding has been attached to the quilt.

Adding a Sleeve Before Binding

To determine the size of the hanging sleeve measure the width of the quilt and add 2" to that measurement. Cut a strip of fabric 8" wide by quilt top measurement taken.

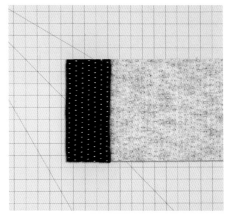

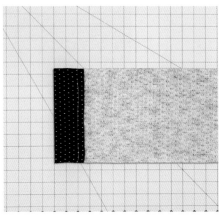

1 Fold under the short edges of the cut strip 1-1/2".

2 Press and sew with a 1/4" seam along the short raw edges.

tip — Check frequently to be sure your stitches are not coming through to the front of the quilt when attaching the hanging sleeve.

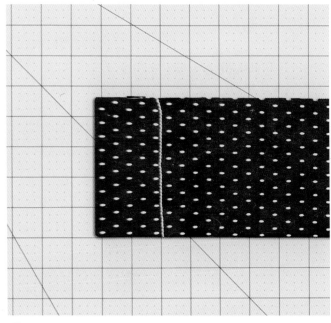

3 Fold the sleeve in half, with long edges and wrong sides together. Press.

FORMULA TO DETERMINE THE SIZE OF HANGING SLEEVE NEEDED:

        ___" (width of quilt)
+   2"
=   ___ (length of fabric strip to cut)
Cut fabric strip 8" wide x length determined above

EXAMPLE TO DETERMINE THE SIZE OF HANGING SLEEVE NEEDED:

    38" (width of quilt)
+   2"
= 40" (length of fabric strip to cut)
Cut fabric strip 8" x 40"

adding a hanging sleeve

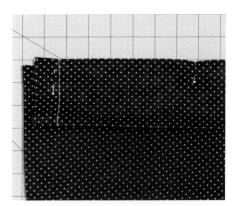

4 Align the raw edges of the sleeve with the top edge of the quilt back. Pin in place. Using a scant 1/4" seam allowance, machine baste the sleeve to the quilt and remove the pins.

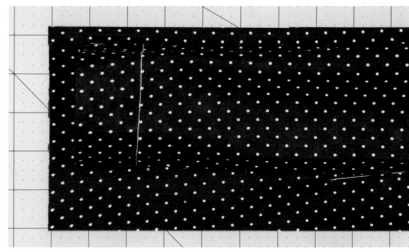

5 Cover the raw edges of the hanging sleeve as you turn the binding to the back of your quilt.

After the binding has been added and turned, fold the bottom long folded edge of the hanging sleeve up approximately 1/2" and hand stitch to the quilt back.

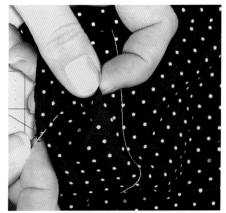

6 Hand stitch the hemmed short edges to the quilt backing where they touch.

tip — Do not stitch the hanging sleeve flat on the quilt back. If you do, the dowel or board inserted into it will form a ridge on the front of the quilt while hanging.

If your quilt is wider than 60" you will need to attach more than one hanging sleeve to allow it to lay flat against the wall.

FORMULA TO DETERMINE THE SIZE OF HANGING SLEEVES NEEDED FOR A 60" OR WIDER QUILT TOP:

	___"	(width of quilt)
+	2"	
=		
÷	3	(number of hanging sleeves)
=	___	**(length** of fabric strips to cut)

Cut three fabric strips 8" wide x length determined above

If you choose to add more hanging sleeves, use the same formula to determine the measurements.

EXAMPLE TO DETERMINE THE SIZE OF HANGING SLEEVES NEEDED FOR A 73" WIDE QUILT TOP:

	73"	(width of quilt)
+	2"	
=	75"	
÷	3	(number of hanging sleeves needed)
=	25"	**(length** of fabric strip to cut)

Cut three fabric strips 8" x 25".

adding a hanging sleeve

Adding a Sleeve After Binding

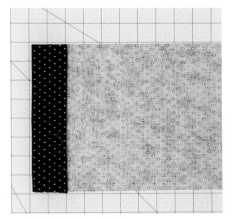

1 Use the formula on page 85 to determine the size of fabric strip to cut for the hanging sleeve. Fold under the short edges of the cut strip 1-1/2".

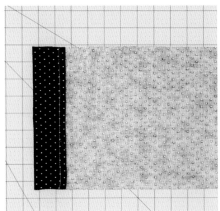

2 Press and sew with a 1/4" seam along the short raw edges.

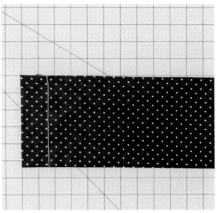

3 Fold the sleeve in half with long edges and wrong sides together.

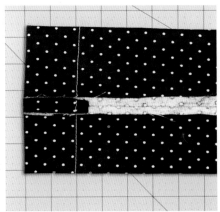

4 Sew the long edges together with a 1/4" seam allowance. Press the seam open.

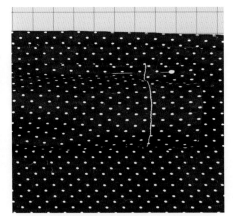

5 Center the seam in the middle of the sleeve and press again. Pin the top edge of the sleeve in place on the quilt back approximately 1" below the top edge of the quilt and with the center seam against the quilt backing. Pull the bottom edge of the hanging sleeve up approximately 1/2" and pin in place. Hand stitch the hanging sleeve to the backing along both long edges.

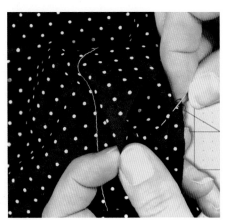

6 Hand stitch the hemmed short edges to the quilt backing where they touch.

tip — The dowel or flat board used for hanging the quilt should be approximately 1" longer than the finished hanging sleeve.

FINISHING THE QUILT
labeling the quilt

It is important to sign and date every quilt you finish. Future generations will appreciate knowing the name of the quiltmaker and the date the quilt was made. In addition to your name and date, you may wish to add the name of the quilt and, if it is a gift, the name of the recipient, as well as the occasion.

Quilts can be labeled in several ways. The quickest and easiest is to sign directly on the quilt with a fine-tip, permanent fabric marking pen. Use a leftover scrap of the quilt's backing fabric to practice writing before signing the actual quilt top.

Embroider your name and the date on the quilt.

Use an extra block from the front of the quilt as a label. Add the block to the quilt back by turning the raw edges under and hand sewing it to the back with an appliqué stitch. The same technique will work to affix a purchased quilt label to your quilt.

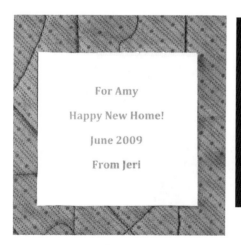

Design a label on your computer and print it on a fabric printer sheet. Check with your local quilt shop to see if it carries these fabric sheets. Follow the manufacturer's instructions when using this method.

tip
When I add labels to the back of my quilts, I press the raw edges under and then cut a piece of lightweight fusible web to cover the inside portion of the label. I affix the fusible web to the back of the label following the manufacturer's instructions and then adhere it to the quilt back. The fusible web holds the label in place while I'm stitching, plus if I don't have time to sew the label on right away I don't have to worry about losing the label or getting stuck with pins.

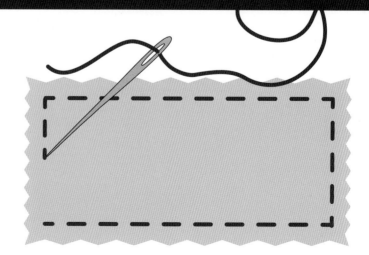

PROJECTS

It's time to take the techniques learned to create your own
quilt or table topper. The projects on the following pages can
be created with the skills you have just mastered. Charts, Formulas,
Quilting Terms and Definitions are also in this section.

table toppers • wallhangings • quilts

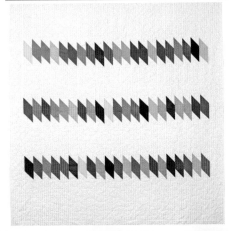

QUILT

Four-Patch Quilt

Finished Size:
48" x 57"

Designed and made by Jeri Simon; quilted by Flying Needle Quilting

four-patch quilt

Materials

1/3 yard medium floral print fabric

1/3 yard gray print fabric

3/4 yard large floral print fabric
Note: You will need more fabric if fussy cutting your squares.

1-3/8 yards black stripe fabric

3-1/2 yards backing fabric

54" x 63" piece of batting

Yardages for 44/45"-wide fabrics.
Sew with 1/4" seam allowance.
wof = width of fabric

Cutting Instructions

From medium floral print fabric, cut:
(3) 3-1/2" x wof strips

From gray print fabric, cut:
(3) 3-1/2" x wof strips

From large floral fabric, fussy cut:
(15) 6-1/2" squares

From black stripe fabric, cut:
(14) 3-1/2" x wof strips.
  From 4 strips, cut:
  (24) 3-1/2" x 6-1/2" block sashing strips.
(6) 2-1/2" x wof binding strips

Making the Four-Patch Blocks

1 Lay out (1) 3-1/2" x wof medium floral print strip and (1) 3-1/2" x wof gray print strip as shown.

2 Sew the strips together along one long edge to make a strip set. Press. Make 3 strip sets.

Make 3

3 Cut the strip sets into 3-1/2"-wide segments. You will need 30.

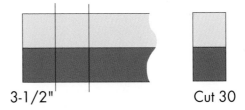

3-1/2"　　　　　　　　Cut 30

4 Lay two segments right sides together with the gray print squares on the medium floral print squares. Match the center seams.

5 Sew the segments together and press open to make a four-patch block. Make 15 four-patch blocks.

Make 15

four-patch quilt

Assembling the Rows

1 Referring to the Row Assembly Diagram, lay out the 6-1/2" large floral squares, four-patch blocks and 3-1/2" x 6-1/2" black stripe block sashing strips in six rows as shown.

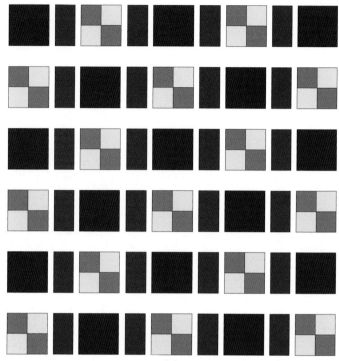

Row Assembly Diagram

2 Sew the pieces together in rows. Press seams toward the block sashing strips.

color option

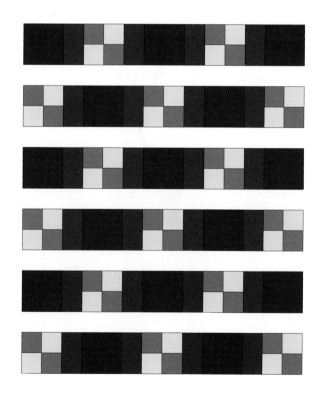

four-patch quilt

Assembling the Quilt Center

1   Referring to the Quilt Center Assembly Diagram, lay out the six block rows and (5) 3-1/2" x wof black stripe strips as shown.

2   Sew the block rows and 3-1/2" x wof strips together. Press seams in one direction.

3   Trim any excess fabric from the 3-1/2" x wof strips to complete the quilt center.

Adding the Borders

1   Sew 3-1/2" x wof black stripe strips to the top and bottom of the quilt center. Press and trim any excess fabric.

2   Sew the remaining (3) 3-1/2" x wof black stripe strips together along the short edges. Press seams open.

3   Measure the quilt length through the center and cut two strips to this length. Sew the strips to opposite sides of the quilt center to complete the quilt top.

Finishing the Quilt

1   Layer the backing, batting, and quilt top. Baste the layers together and hand or machine quilt.

2   Sew (6) 2-1/2" x wof black stripe binding strips together using diagonal seams to create one continuous binding strip. Press the strip in half, wrong sides together, along the length. Sew binding to the edges of the quilt.

3   Trim the extra batting and backing even with the quilt top. Turn the binding over the edge to the back and hand or machine sew in place.

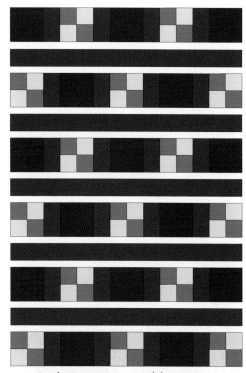

Quilt Center Assembly Diagram

QUILT

Strip Quilt

Finished Size:
58-1/2" x 66"

Designed and made by Jeri Simon; quilted by Flying Needle Quilting

strip quilt

Materials

2-1/4 yards assorted medium to dark fabrics OR 1 bundle of precut 2-1/2" strips

2-1/4 yards assorted light fabrics OR 1 bundle of precut 2-1/2" strips

4-1/4 yards backing fabric

65" x 72" piece of batting

Yardages for 44/45"-wide fabrics.
Sew with 1/4" seam allowance.
wof = width of fabric

Cutting Instructions

From assorted medium to dark fabrics, cut:
(27) 2-1/2" x wof strips

From assorted light fabrics, cut:
(27) 2-1/2" x wof strips

From remaining light and medium to dark fabrics, cut:
(7) 2-1/2" x wof binding strips

Making the Segments

Note: Separate the strips into stacks of lights and darks

1 Lay out (2) 2-1/2" x wof light strips and (1) 2-1/2" x wof dark strip as shown.

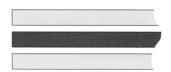

2 Sew the strips together along the long edges to make a light/dark/light strip set. Make 9 light/dark/light strip sets.

Make 9

3 Lay out (2) 2-1/2" x wof dark strips and (1) 2-1/2" x wof light strip as shown.

4 Sew the strips together along the long edges to make a dark/light/dark strip set. Make 9 dark/light/dark strip sets.

Make 9

5 Cut 6 light/dark/light strip sets and 6 dark/light/dark strip sets into 2-1/2" x 20-1/2" segments. You will need (11) 2-1/2" x 20-1/2" light/dark/light segments and (11) 2-1/2" x 20-1/2" dark/light/dark segments.

6 Cut 3 light/dark/light strip sets and 3 dark/light/dark strip sets into 2-1/2" x 16-1/2" segments. You will need (6) 2-1/2" x 16-1/2" light/dark/light segments and (6) 2-1/2" x 16-1/2" dark/light/dark segments.

strip quilt

Assembling the Quilt

1 Lay out (6) 2-1/2" x 20-1/2" dark/light/dark segments and (5) 2-1/2" x 20-1/2" light/dark/light segments as shown.

2 Sew the segments together along the long edges to make row A.

Row A

3 Lay out (6) 2-1/2" x 20-1/2" light/dark/light segments and (5) 2-1/2" x 20-1/2" dark/light/dark segments as shown.

4 Sew the segments together along the long edges to make row B.

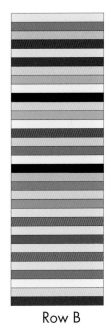

Row B

96

strip quilt

5 Lay out (2) 2-1/2" x 16-1/2" dark/light/dark segments and (2) 2-1/2" x 16-1/2" light/dark/light segments as shown.

6 Sew the segments together along the short edges to make a sashing row. Make 3 sashing rows.

7 Referring to the Quilt Assembly Diagram, lay out the sashing rows, row A and row B.

8 Sew the rows together.

9 Trim the sashing rows even with rows A and B to complete the quilt top.

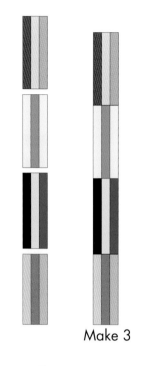

Make 3

Finishing the Quilt

1 Layer the backing, batting, and quilt top. Baste the layers together and hand or machine quilt.

2 Sew (7) 2-1/2" x wof binding strips together using diagonal seams to create one continuous binding strip. Press the strip in half, wrong sides together, along the length. Sew binding to the edges of the quilt.

3 Trim the extra batting and backing even with the quilt top. Turn the binding over the edge to the back and hand or machine sew in place.

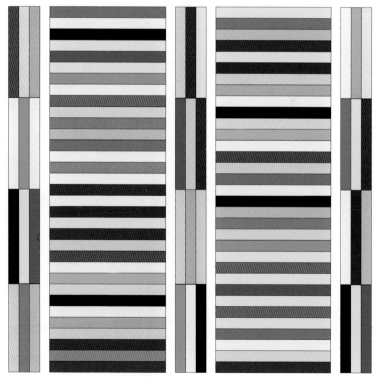

Quilt Assembly Diagram

TABLE RUNNER

Pinwheel Table Runner

Finished Size:
16" x 37-1/4"

Designed, made, and quilted by Sue Voegtlin

pinwheel table runner

Materials

1/4 yard cream print fabric

1/4 yard black with cream circles fabric

3/8 yard black print fabric

3/8 yard stripe fabric

1/4 yard black line print fabric

3/4 yard backing fabric

22" x 44" piece batting

Yardages for 44/45"-wide fabrics.
Sew with 1/4" seam allowance.
wof = width of fabric

Cutting Instructions

From cream print fabric, cut:
(1) 4-5/8" x wof strip. From the strip, cut:
  (6) 4-5/8" squares.

From black with cream circles fabric, cut:
(1) 4-5/8"" x wof strip. From the strip, cut:
  (6) 4-5/8" squares.

From black print fabric, cut:
(1) 12" square; cut the square into quarters
  diagonally to make 4 setting triangles.
(2) 6-1/4" squares; cut the squares in
  half diagonally to make 4 corner triangles.

From stripe fabric, cut:
(3) 3" x wof strips. From 1 strip, cut:
  (2) 3" x 20" border strips. The remaining
  strips will also be used for borders.

From black line print fabric, cut:
(3) 2-1/2" x wof binding strips

From backing fabric, cut:
(1) 22" x 44" rectangle

Assembling the Pinwheel Blocks

1 Draw a diagonal line on the wrong side of the 4-5/8" cream print squares as shown.

2 With right sides together, layer the 4-5/8" cream print squares on the 4-5/8" black with cream circles squares. Sew 1/4" on either side of the drawn lines.

3 Cut on the drawn line between the stitching as shown. Press seams toward the black with cream circles fabric. The half-square triangle blocks should measure 4-1/4" square.

4 Arrange groups of four half-square triangle blocks. Sew the half-square triangles together in rows.

5 Sew the rows together to make a pinwheel block. Make 3 pinwheel blocks.

Make 3

pinwheel table runner

Assembling the Table Runner Center

1 Lay out the pinwheel blocks and 4 black print setting triangles on a flat surface.

2 Sew the blocks and setting triangles together in diagonal rows. Press the seam allowances toward the setting triangles.

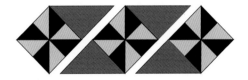

3 Sew the rows together; press seams in one direction.

4 Add black print corner triangles to complete the table runner top. Press seams toward the corner triangles.

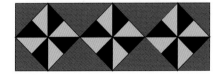

Adding the Border

1 Center and sew a 3" x 20" stripe border strip to one short edge of the table runner center, beginning and ending the seam 1/4" from the corners of the runner center. Repeat on the opposite edge of the runner center.

2 Center and sew a 3" x wof stripe strip to the remaining edges in the same manner. Press seams toward the border.

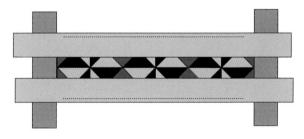

3 Place the table runner right side up on an ironing board. Working with one corner at a time, extend the border ends out so the vertical strip overlaps the horizontal strip.

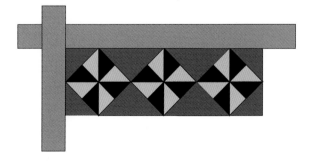

pinwheel table runner

4 Lift up the vertical strip and fold it under itself at a 45-degree angle. Check the angle with a ruler and press.

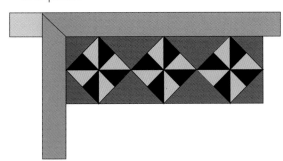

5 With right sides together, fold the table topper on the diagonal so the edges of the two border strips line up. Pin and sew along the creased line from the inner point where the previous stitching ends to the outer edge of the border, backstitching to secure. Trim seam to 1/4". Press seam allowance open.

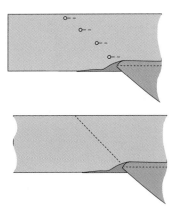

6 Repeats steps 3 - 5 for the remaining corners.

Finishing the Table Runner

1 Layer the backing, batting, and table runner top. Baste the layers together and hand or machine quit as desired.

2 Sew (3) 2-1/2" x wof binding strips together using diagonal seams to create one continuous binding strip. Press the strip in half, wrong sides together, along the length. Sew binding to the edges of the table runner.

3 Trim the extra batting and backing even with the table runner top. Turn the binding over the edge to the back and hand or machine sew in place.

WALLHANGING

Triangle Star Wallhanging

Finished Size:
28" x 28"

Designed by Shirley Harrison; made and quilted by Jeri Simon

triangle star wallhanging

Materials

1 yard leaf print fabric

1/3 yard purple fabric

1/4 yard red fabric

1/4 yard yellow-green fabric

1/8 yard green fabric

1 yard backing fabric

34" x 34" piece of batting

Yardages for 44/45"-wide fabrics.
Sew with 1/4" seam allowance.
wof = width of fabric

Cutting Instructions

From leaf print fabric, cut:
(1) 15" x wof strip. From the strip, cut:
  (2) 15" squares. Cut the squares in half
  diagonally to make 4 corner triangles.
(1) 5-1/2" x wof strip. From the strip, cut:
  (5) 5-1/2" squares.
(1) 3" x wof strip. From the strip, cut:
  (4) 3" squares.
(3) 2-1/2" x wof binding strips

From purple fabric, cut:
(1) 3-3/8" x wof strip. From the strip, cut:
  (6) 3-3/8" squares.
(2) 3" x wof strips. From the strips, cut:
  (16) 3" squares.

From red fabric, cut:
(1) 3-3/8" x wof strip. From the strip, cut:
  (6) 3-3/8" squares.
(1) 3" x wof strip. From the strip, cut:
  (12) 3" squares.

From yellow-green fabric, cut:
(2) 3" x wof strips. From the strips, cut:
  (8) 3" x 5-1/2" rectangles.
(12) 3" squares

From green fabric, cut:
(1) 3" x wof strip. From the strip, cut:
  (8) 3" squares.

From backing fabric, cut:
(1) 34" square

Making the Square-in-a-Square Units

1 Draw a diagonal line on the wrong side of (8) 3" green squares, (8) 3" purple squares and (4) 3" red squares as shown.

2 With right sides together, place a 3" green square and a 3" purple square on opposite corners of a 5-1/2" leaf print square. Sew on the drawn lines. Trim the seam allowances to 1/4" and press toward the outside corners.

3 Place a 3" green square and a 3" red square on the remaining corners of the 5-1/2" leaf print square. Sew on the drawn lines. Trim the seam allowances to 1/4" and press to make a square-in-a-square unit. Make a total of 4 square-in-a-square units. The units should measure 5-1/2".

Make 4

triangle star wallhanging

4 Use the remaining 5-1/2" leaf print square and (4) 3" purple squares to make the center square-in-a-square unit in the same manner.

Making the Corner Units

1 Draw a diagonal line on the wrong side of a 3-3/8" red square. With right sides together, layer the 3-3/8" red square on a 3-3/8" purple square.

2 Sew 1/4" on either side of the drawn line. Cut on the drawn line as shown. Press seam toward the purple fabric. Make a total of 12 half-square triangle blocks. Each block should measure 3" square.

Make 12

3 Lay out 3 half-square triangle blocks and a 3" leaf print square as shown. Sew the pieces together in pairs, pressing the seams in alternating directions. Sew the pairs together to complete one corner unit. Press seams in one direction. Make a total of 4 corner units. The corner units should measure 5-1/2" square.

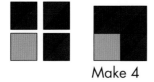

Make 4

Making the Flying Geese Units

1 Draw a diagonal line on the wrong side of (8) 3" red squares and (8) 3" purple squares as shown.

2 With right sides together, lay a 3" red square on the right end of a 3" x 5-1/2" yellow-green rectangle as shown. Sew on the drawn line and trim the seam allowance to 1/4". Press the seams toward the red triangle.

3 Sew a 3" purple square to the opposite end of the rectangle in the same manner to make a flying geese unit. Make a total of 8 flying geese units. The flying geese units should measure 3" x 5-1/2".

Make 8

Assembling the Wallhanging

1 Lay out 5 square-in-a-square units and 4 corner units as shown.

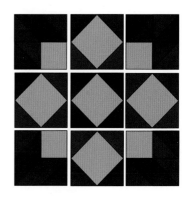

triangle star wallhanging

2 Sew the units together in horizontal rows. Press the seams of each row to one side, alternating the direction with each row. Sew the rows together. Press the seams in one direction.

3 Lay out 2 flying geese units and (2) 3" yellow-green squares as shown. Sew the pieces together to make a flying geese row. Make a total of 4 flying geese rows.

Make 4

4 Sew 2 flying geese rows to opposite edges of the wallhanging center. Press seams toward the flying geese rows.

5 Add 3" yellow-green squares to each end of the 2 remaining flying geese rows. Press seams away from the flying geese units. Sew these to the remaining edges to complete the wallhanging center.

6 Sew a leaf print corner triangle to each edge of the wallhanging center. Press seams toward the triangles.

Finishing the Wallhanging

1 Layer the backing, batting, and wallhanging top. Baste the layers together and hand or machine quilt.

2 Sew (3) 2-1/2" x wof binding strips together using diagonal seams to create one continuous binding strip. Press the strip in half, wrong sides together, along the length. Sew binding to the edges of the wallhanging.

3 Trim the extra batting and backing even with the wallhanging top. Turn the binding over the edge to the back and hand or machine sew in place.

TABLE TOPPER

Flying Geese Table Topper

Finished Size:
28-1/2" x 28-1/2"

Designed and made by Jeri Simon; quilted by Sharon Hart

flying geese table topper

Materials

1/2 yard black print fabric

3/4 yard orange fabric

5/8 yard turquoise fabric

1 yard backing fabric

34" x 34" piece of batting

Yardages for 44/45"-wide fabrics.
Sew with 1/4" seam allowance.
wof = width of fabric

Cutting Instructions

From black print fabric, fussy cut:
(4) 8-1/2" squares
(3) 2-1/2" x wof binding strips

From orange fabric, cut:
(9) 2-1/2" x wof strips.
   From the strips, cut:
   (132) 2-1/2" squares.

From turquoise fabric, cut:
(8) 2-1/2" x wof strips.
   From the strips, cut:
   (66) 2-1/2" x 4-1/2" rectangles.

From backing fabric, cut:
(1) 34" square

Making the Flying Geese Units

1 Draw a diagonal line on the wrong side of the (132) 2-1/2" orange squares as shown.

2 With right sides together, align a 2-1/2" orange square on the right end of a 2-1/2" x 4-1/2" turquoise rectangle as shown. Sew on the drawn line and trim the seam allowances to 1/4". Press seams toward the orange triangle.

3 Sew another 2-1/2" orange square to the opposite end of the rectangle in the same manner to make a flying geese unit as shown.

4 Repeat Steps 1 - 3 to make a total of 66 flying geese units. The flying geese units should measure 2-1/2" x 4-1/2".

flying geese table topper

Assembling the Table Topper Center

1   Sew flying geese units together to make 2 rows of 5 units and 2 rows of 4 units for the sashing strips as shown. Press seams in one direction.

Make 2   **Make 2**

2   Lay out the (4) 8-1/2" black print blocks and the 5-unit and 4-unit sashing strips as shown.

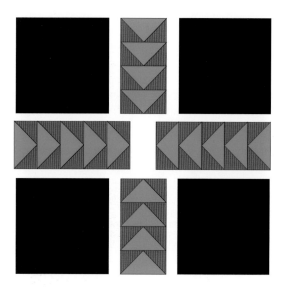

3   Sew the blocks and 4-unit sashing strips together in horizontal rows. Press seams away from the sashing strips.

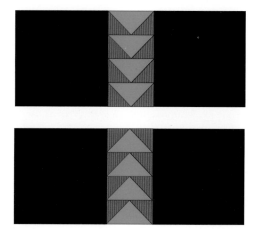

4   Join the two 5-unit sashing strips to make a 10-unit sashing strip as shown. Press seams in one direction.

5   Sew the block rows together with the 10-unit sashing strip. Press seams away from the sashing strip.

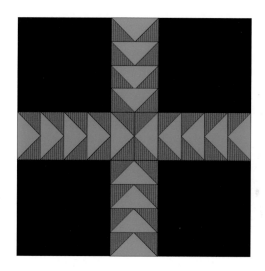

flying geese table topper

Adding the Border

1 Join flying geese units to make 2 rows of ten units for the top and bottom border strips. Press seams in one direction.

Make 2

2 Sew a border strip to the top and bottom edges of the table topper center. Press seams away from the center.

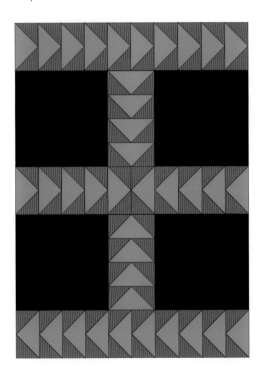

3 Sew together the remaining flying geese units in 2 rows of 12 units and 2 pairs. Press seams in one direction.

Make 2

Make 2

4 Add 1 pair of flying geese to the left end of each 12-unit strip as shown for the side border strips. Press seams toward the pairs.

5 Add the side border strips to the left and right edges of the table topper center. Press seams away from the center.

Finishing the Table Topper

1 Layer the backing, batting, and table topper top. Baste the layers together and hand or machine quilt as desired.

2 Sew (3) 2-1/2" x wof binding strips together using diagonal seams to create one continuous binding strip. Press the strip in half, wrong sides together, along the length. Sew binding to the edges of the wallhanging.

3 Trim the extra batting and backing even with the edges of the table topper top. Turn the binding over the edge to the back and hand or machine sew in place.

NAP THROW

Hungry Caterpillar Nap Throw

Finished Size:
33-1/2" x 36-1/2"

Designed and made by Jeri Simon; quilted by Sharon Hart

hungry caterpillar nap throw

Materials

23-1/2" x 26-1/2" pre-printed panel

3/8 yard green fabric

1/2 yard gold fabric

3/4 yard purple fabric

1-1/4 yards backing fabric

40" x 43" piece of batting

Yardages are for 44/45"-wide fabrics.
Sew with 1/4" seam allowance.
wof = width of fabric

Cutting Instructions

From green fabric, cut:
(4)-1/2" x wof strips.
  From the strips, cut:
  (2) 2-1/2" x 23-1/2" inner border strips.
  (2) 2-1/2" x 30-1/2" inner border strips.

From gold fabric, cut:
(3) 4-1/2" x wof strips.
  From the strips, cut:
  (21) 4-1/2" squares. Cut the squares into quarters diagonally to make 84 triangles.

From purple fabric, cut:
(3) 4-1/2" x wof strips.
  From the strips, cut:
  (21) 4-1/2" squares. Cut the squares into quarters diagonally to make 84 triangles.
(4) 2-1/2" x wof binding strips

From backing fabric, cut:
(1) 40" x 43" rectangle

Making the Hourglass Units

1 Arrange 2 gold and 2 purple triangles as shown. Sew the triangles together in pairs. Press seams in opposite directions.

2 Sew the pairs together to complete one hourglass unit. Press seams in one direction. Make a total of 42 hourglass units. The hourglass units should measure 3-1/2" square.

Make 42

color option

The panel is the focus fabric (page 14) in this project. I pulled out the purple and gold to make the hourglass blocks in the border, but any of the colors shown here would have worked just as well.

hungry caterpillar nap throw

Assembling the Throw Top

1 Sew the 2-1/2" x 23-1/2" green inner border strips to the top and bottom edges of the pre-printed panel. Press seams toward the border.

2 Sew the 2-1/2" x 30-1/2" green inner border strips to the left and right edges of the pre-printed panel. Press seams toward the border.

3 Join 9 hourglass units to make top outer border strip as shown. Press seams in one direction. Repeat for bottom border strip.

Make 2

hungry caterpillar nap throw

4 Sew a border strip to the top and bottom edges of the quilt center. Press seams toward the center.

5 Sew together the remaining hourglass units in 2 rows of 12 units as shown for the side borders. Press seams in one direction.

Make 2

6 Add the side border strips to the left and right edges of the quilt center. Press seams toward the center.

Finishing the Throw

1 Layer the backing, batting, and throw top. Baste the layers together and hand or machine quilt as desired.

2 Sew (4) 2-1/2" x wof binding strips together using diagonal seams to create one continuous binding strip. Press the strip in half, wrong sides together, along the length. Sew binding to the edges of the throw.

3 Trim the extra batting and backing even with the edges of the throw top. Turn the binding over the edges to the back and hand or machine sew in place.

QUILT

Diagonal Diamonds Quilt

Finished Size:
48" x 58"

Designed and made by Jeri Simon; quilted by Flying Needle Quilting

diagonal diamonds quilt

Materials

3-1/8 yards white print fabric

7/8 yard total assorted solid fabrics

3-1/2 yards backing fabric

54" x 64" piece of batting

Yardages for 44/45"-wide fabrics.
Sew with 1/4" seam allowance.
wof = width of fabric

Cutting Instructions

From white print fabric, cut:
(34) 2-1/2" x wof strips.
   From 28 strips, cut:
   (84) 2-1/2" x 12" strips.
   Note: The remaining strips will be
   used for binding.
(3) 3-1/2" x wof strips for side borders
(3) 5" x wof strips for top and bottom borders

From assorted solid fabrics, cut:
(11) 2-1/2" x wof strips.
   From the strips, cut:
   (63) 2-1/2" x 6" strips.

Assembling the Rows

1 Lay a 2-1/2" x 12" white print strip right side up on a flat surface. Place a 2-1/2" x 6" solid strip, wrong side up and perpendicular on the white strip.

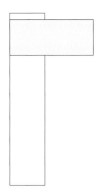

2 Draw a diagonal line from corner to corner on the wrong side of the solid strip.

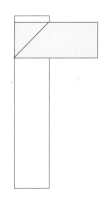

3 Sew on the drawn line and trim 1/4" from the sewn line.

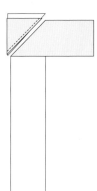

diagonal diamonds quilt

4 Press the seam open.

5 Following steps 1 - 4, sew an additional 3 white strips and 2 solid strips to the unit to complete the row. Make 21 rows.

color option

Make 21

diagonal diamonds quilt

Assembling the Quilt Center

1 Referring to the Quilt Assembly Diagram, lay out the rows.

2 Sew the rows together to complete the quilt center.

Adding the Borders

1 Sew the (3) 3-1/2" x wof strips together along the short edges. Press seams open.

2 Sew the strip to one side of the quilt center. Press the seam open and trim the strip even with the quilt center.

3 Sew the remaining portion of the strip to the opposite side of the quilt center. Press the seam open and trim the strip even with the quilt center.

4 Referring to step 1, sew the (3) 5" x wof strips together.

5 Referring to steps 2 - 3, sew the strip to the top and bottom of the quilt center to complete the quilt top.

Finishing the Quilt

1 Layer the backing, batting, and quilt top. Baste the layers together and hand or machine quilt.

2 Sew the remaining 2-1/2" x wof white binding strips together using diagonal seams to create one continuous binding strip. Press the strip in half, wrong sides together, along the length. Sew binding to the edges of the quilt.

3 Trim the extra batting and backing even with the quilt top. Turn the binding over the edge to the back and hand or machine sew in place.

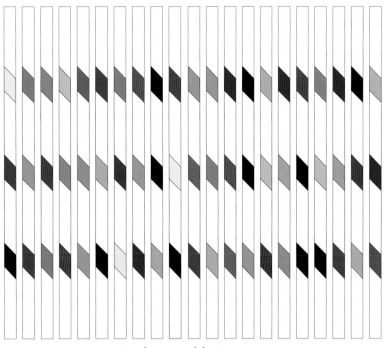

Quilt Assembly Diagram

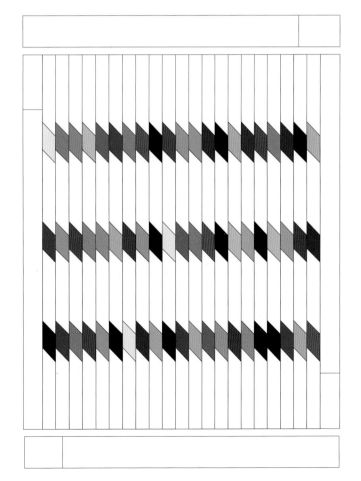

CHARTS

REDUCING AND ENLARGING BLOCKS

When reducing or enlarging a quilt block a photocopy machine is a helpful tool. Always double-check the measurements of the final image after reducing or enlarging it on the photocopy machine. Another useful tool when figuring block size reduction or enlargement is a Proportional Scale tool. It resembles a wheel and can be found at quilt, art, or craft stores.

Enlarging a block
If you have a 6-inch block that you would like to make into a 12-inch block follow this formula:
12 (desired size) ÷ 6 (original size) x 100 = 200% (enlargement)

Reducing a block
If you have a 6-inch block that you would like to make into a 4-inch block follow this formula:
4 (desired size) ÷ 6 (original size) x 100 = 66.6% (reduction)

Refer to the charts provided for more samples on reducing and enlarging blocks.

Original Finished Block Size	Desired Finished Block Size — 2" to 7-1/2"											
	2"	2-1/2"	3"	3-1/2"	4"	4-1/2"	5"	5-1/2"	6"	6-1/2"	7"	7-1/2"
2"	100%	125%	150%	175%	200%	225%	250%	275%	300%	325%	350%	375%
2-1/2"	80%	100%	120%	140%	160%	180%	200%	220%	240%	260%	280%	300%
3"	66.6%	120%	100%	116.6%	133.3%	150%	166.6%	183.3%	200%	216.6%	233.3%	250%
3-1/2"	57.1%	71.4%	85.7%	100%	114.2%	128.5%	142.8%	157.1%	171.4%	185.7%	200%	214.2%
4"	50%	62.5%	75%	87.5%	100%	112.5%	125%	137.5%	150%	162.5%	175%	187.5%
4-1/2"	44.4%	55.5%	66.6%	77.7%	88.8%	100%	111.1%	122.2%	133.3%	144.4%	155.5%	166.6%
5"	40%	50%	60%	70%	80%	90%	100%	110%	120%	130%	140%	150%
5-1/2"	36.3%	45.4%	54.5%	63.6%	72.7%	81.8%	90.9%	100%	109%	118.1%	127.2%	136.3%
6"	33.3%	41.6%	50%	58.3%	66.6%	75%	83.3%	91.6%	100%	108.3%	116.6%	125%
6-1/2"	30.7%	38.4%	46.1%	53.8%	61.5%	69.2%	76.9%	84.6%	92.3%	100%	107.6%	115.3%
7"	28.5%	35.7%	42.8%	50%	57.1%	64.2%	71.4%	78.5%	85.7%	92.8%	100%	107.1%
7-1/2"	26.6%	33.3%	40%	46.6%	53.3%	60%	66.6%	73.3%	80%	86.6%	93.3%	100%
8"	25%	31.2%	37.5%	43.7%	50%	56.2%	62.5%	68.7%	75%	81.2%	87.5%	93.7%
8-1/2"	23.5%	29.4%	35.2%	41.1%	47%	52.9%	58.8%	64.7%	70.5%	76.4%	82.3%	88.2%
9"	22.2%	27.7%	33.3%	38.8%	44.4%	50%	55.5%	61.1%	66.6%	72.2%	77.7%	83.3%
9-1/2"	21%	26.3%	31.5%	36.8%	42.1%	47.3%	52.6%	57.8%	63.1%	68.4%	73.6%	78.9%
10"	20%	25%	30%	35%	40%	45%	50%	55%	60%	65%	70%	75%
10-1/2"	19%	23.8%	28.5%	33.3%	38%	42.8%	47.6%	52.3%	57.1%	61.9%	66.6%	71.4%
11"	18.1%	22.7%	27.2%	31.8%	36.3%	40.9%	45.4%	50%	54.5%	59%	63.6%	68.1%
11-1/2"	17.3%	21.7%	26%	30.4%	34.7%	39.1%	43.4%	47.8%	52.1%	56.5%	60.8%	65.2%
12"	16.6%	20.8%	25%	29.1%	33.3%	37.5%	41.6%	45.8%	50%	54.1%	58.3%	62.5%

Desired Finished Block Sizes 8" to 12" on page 119.

REDUCING AND ENLARGING BLOCKS

Desired Finished Block Size — 8" to 12"

Original Finished Block Size	8"	8-1/2	9"	9-1/2"	10"	10-1/2"	11"	11-1/2"	12"
2"	400%	425%	450%	475%	500%	525%	550%	575%	600%
2-1/2"	320%	340%	360%	380%	400%	420%	440%	460%	480%
3"	266.6%	283.3%	300%	316.6%	333.3%	350%	366.6%	383.3%	400%
3-1/2"	228.5%	242.8%	257.1%	271.4%	285.7%	300%	314.2%	328.5%	342.8%
4"	200%	212.5%	225%	237.5%	250%	262.5%	275%	287.5%	300%
4-1/2"	177.7%	188.8%	200%	211.1%	222.2%	233.3%	244.4%	255.5%	266.6%
5"	160%	170%	180%	190%	200%	210%	220%	230%	240%
5-1/2"	145.4%	154.5%	163.6%	172.7%	181.8%	190.9%	200%	209%	218.1%
6"	133.3%	141.6%	150%	158.3%	166.6%	175%	183.3%	191.6%	200%
6-1/2"	123%	130.7%	138.4%	146.1%	153.8%	161.5%	169.2%	176.9%	184.6%
7"	114.2%	121.4%	128.5%	135.7%	142.8%	150%	157.1%	164.2%	171.4%
7-1/2"	106.6%	113.3%	120%	126.6%	133.3%	140%	146.6%	153.3%	160%
8"	100%	106.2%	112.5%	118.7%	125%	131.2%	137.5%	143.7%	150%
8-1/2"	94.1%	100%	105.8%	111.7%	117.6%	123.5%	129.4%	135.2%	141.1%
9"	88.8%	94.4%	100%	105.5%	111.1%	116.6%	122.2%	127.7%	133.3%
9-1/2"	84.2%	89.4%	94.7%	100%	105.2%	110.5%	115.7%	121%	126.3%
10"	80%	85%	90%	95%	100%	105%	110%	115%	120%
10-1/2"	76.1%	80.9%	85.7%	90.4%	95.2%	100%	104.7%	109.5%	114.2%
11"	72.7%	77.2%	81.8%	86.3%	90.9%	95.4%	100%	104.5%	109%
11-1/2"	69.5%	73.9%	78.2%	82.6%	86.9%	91.3%	95.6%	100%	104.3%
12"	66.6%	70.8%	75%	79.1%	83.3%	87.5%	91.6%	95.8%	100%

CONVERTING YARDS TO INCHES TO DECIMALS TO METRES

1/8 yard	=	4-1/2 inches	=	.125 decimals	=	.114 metres
1/4 yard	=	9 inches	=	.25 decimals	=	.229 metres
1/3 yard	=	12 inches	=	.333 decimals	=	.304 metres
3/8 yard	=	13-1/2 inches	=	.375 decimals	=	.343 metres
1/2 yard	=	18 inches	=	.50 decimals	=	.457 metres
5/8 yard	=	22-1/2 inches	=	.625 decimals	=	.572 metres
2/3 yard	=	24 inches	=	.666 decimals	=	.610 metres
3/4 yard	=	27 inches	=	.75 decimals	=	.686 metres
7/8 yard	=	31-1/2 inches	=	.875 decimals	=	.8 metres
1 yard	=	36 inches	=	1.00 decimals	=	.914 metres
Fat Eighth	=	9 x 22 inches	=	.25 x .575 decimals	=	.229 x .56 metres
Fat Quarter	=	18 x 22 inches	=	.50 x .575 decimals	=	.457 x .56 metres

NUMBER OF SQUARES FROM SPECIFIC FABRIC YARDAGE

Size of Squares	Fabric Yardage							
	1/4 yard	1/2 yard	3/4 yard	1 yard	1-1/4 yards	1-1/2 yards	1-3/4 yards	2 yards
2"	80	180	260	360	440	540	620	720
2-1/2"	48	112	160	224	288	336	400	448
3"	39	78	117	156	195	236	273	312
3-1/2"	22	44	77	110	132	165	198	220
4"	20	40	60	90	110	130	150	180
4-1/2"	18	36	54	72	90	108	126	144
5"	8	24	40	56	72	80	96	112
5-1/2"	7	21	28	42	56	63	77	91
6"	6	18	24	36	42	54	60	72
6-1/2"	6	12	24	30	36	48	54	66
7"	5	10	15	25	30	35	45	60
7-1/2"	5	10	15	20	30	35	40	45
8"	5	10	15	20	25	30	35	45
8-1/2"	4	8	12	16	20	24	28	32
9"	4	8	12	16	20	24	28	32
9-1/2"	x	4	8	12	16	20	24	28
10"	x	4	8	12	16	20	24	28
10-1/2"	x	3	6	9	12	18	15	18
11"	x	3	6	9	12	12	15	18
11-1/2"	x	3	6	9	9	12	15	18
12"	x	3	6	9	9	12	15	18

Number of squares is based on 42"-wide fabric. You may get more squares if using 44"-wide fabric. Remove the selvages before cutting your squares.

STANDARD MATTRESS AND QUILT SIZES

	Crib	Youth	Twin	Full	Queen	King
Mattress Size	27"x 52"	32" x 66"	39" x 75"	54" x 75"	60" x 80"	76" x 80"
Quilt (will cover mattress)	36" x 60"	56" x 78"	63" x 87"	78" x 87"	84" x 92"	106" x 98"
Bedspread (will cover bed with drop close to floor)	NA	74" x 97"	81" x 1 06"	96" x 106"	102" x 111"	120" x 115"

When making a quilt for a specific bed, measure the mattress and determine how much of a drop you want.

NUMBER OF HALF-SQUARE TRIANGLES FROM SPECIFIC FABRIC YARDAGE

Finished Triangle Size	Width of Strip	Fabric Yardage							
		1/4 yard	1/2 yard	3/4 yard	1 yard	1-1/4 yards	1-1/2 yards	1-3/4 yards	2 yards
2"	2-7/8"	84	168	252	336	420	504	588	700
2-1/2"	3-3/8"	48	120	192	240	312	384	432	504
3"	3-7/8"	40	80	120	180	220	260	320	360
3-1/2"	4-3/8"	36	72	108	144	180	216	252	288
4"	4-7/8"	16	48	80	112	144	176	192	224
4-1/2"	5-3/8"	14	42	70	84	112	140	154	182
5"	5-7/8"	14	42	56	84	98	126	140	168
5-1/2"	6-3/8"	12	24	48	60	84	96	108	132
6"	6-7/8"	12	24	36	60	72	84	108	120
6-1/2"	7-3/8"	10	20	30	40	60	70	80	90
7"	7-7/8"	10	20	30	40	50	60	80	90
7-1/2"	8-3/8"	10	20	30	40	50	60	70	80
8"	8-7/8"	8	16	24	32	40	48	56	64
8-1/2"	9-3/8"	x	8	16	24	32	40	48	56
9"	9-7/8"	x	8	16	24	32	40	48	56
9-1/2"	10-3/8"	x	8	16	24	32	40	48	48
10"	10-7/8"	x	6	12	18	24	24	30	36
10-1/2"	11-3/8"	x	6	12	18	18	24	30	36
11"	11-7/8"	x	6	12	18	18	24	30	36
11-1/2"	12-3/8"	x	6	12	12	18	24	30	30
12"	12-7/8"	x	6	12	12	18	24	24	30

Number of triangles is based on 42"-long strips.
Remove the selvages before cutting. A 1/4" seam allowance is included.

NUMBER OF STRIPS FROM FAT QUARTERS (18" x 22")

Size of Strips	Number of Strips
2"	8
2-1/2"	6
3"	6
3-1/2"	5
4"	4
4-1/2"	4
5"	3
5-1/2"	3
6"	3
6-1/2"	2

Number of strips is based on straightening your fabric and removing the selvages before cutting.

NUMBER OF SQUARES FROM FAT QUARTERS (18" x 22")

Size of Squares	Number of Squares
2"	99
2-1/2"	56
3"	42
3-1/2"	30
4"	20
4-1/2"	16
5"	12
5-1/2"	12
6"	9
6-1/2"	6

SETTING BLOCKS

When determining the measurement of a setting block, add 1/2" to the finished block size. This will allow for 1/4" seam allowances.

Setting Block Size	Finished Block Size
2-1/2"	2"
3"	2-1/2"
3-1/2"	3"
4"	3-1/2"
4-1/2"	4"
5"	4-1/2"
5-1/2"	5"
6"	5-1/2"
6-1/2"	6"
7"	6-1/2"
7-1/2"	7"
8"	7-1/2"
8-1/2"	8"
9"	8-1/2"
9-1/2"	9"
10"	9-1/2"
10-1/2"	10"
11"	10-1/2"
11-1/2"	11"
12"	11-1/2"
12-1/2"	12"

HALF-SQUARE TRIANGLE BLOCKS

When figuring the dimension of a half-square triangle block, add 7/8" to both the height and the length of the desired finished size half-square triangle block.

Half-Square Triangles, Cut Block	Finished Block Size
2-7/8"	2"
3-3/8"	2-1/2"
3-7/8"	3"
4-3/8"	3-1/2"
4-7/8"	4"
5-3/8"	4-1/2"
5-7/8"	5"
6-3/8"	5-1/2"
6-7/8"	6"
7-3/8"	6-1/2"
7-7/8"	7"
8-3/8"	7-1/2"
8-7/8"	8"
9-3/8"	8-1/2"
9-7/8"	9"
10-3/8"	9-1/2"
10-7/8"	10"
11-3/8"	10-1/2"
11-7/8"	11"
12-3/8"	11-1/2"
12-7/8"	12"

QUARTER-SQUARE TRIANGLE BLOCKS

When figuring the dimension of a quarter-square triangle block, add 1-1/4" to the desired finished size of the longest side of the quarter-square triangle.

Quarter-Square Triangles, Cut Block	Finished Block Size
3-1/4"	2"
3-3/4"	2-1/2"
4-1/4"	3"
4-3/4"	3-1/2"
5-1/4"	4"
5-3/4"	4-1/2"
6-1/4"	5"
6-3/4"	5-1/2"
7-1/4"	6"
7-3/4"	6-1/2"
8-1/4"	7"
8-3/4"	7-1/2"
9-1/4"	8"
9-3/4"	8-1/2"
10-1/4"	9"
10-3/4"	9-1/2"
11-1/4"	10"
11-3/4"	10-1/2"
12-1/4"	11"
12-3/4"	11-1/2"
13-1/4"	12"

Formulas

FORMULA TO DETERMINE THE LENGTH OF MITERED BORDERS:

Top and bottom border strips

    ___" (quilt top width)
+ ___" (width of two border strips)
+ 1/2" (seam allowance)
+ 6" (just in case)
= ___" top and bottom border strips

Side border strips

    ___" (quilt top length)
+ ___" (width of two border strips)
+ 1/2" (seam allowance)
+ 6" (just in case)
= ___" side border strips

FORMULA TO DETERMINE THE NUMBER OF SCALLOPS ON QUILT TOP:

Top and bottom scallops

    ___" (quilt top width)
÷ ___" (width of scallops)
= ___ top and bottom scallops

Side scallops

    ___" (quilt top length)
÷ ___" (width of scallops)
= ___ side scallops

DIAGONAL BLOCK MEASUREMENTS

When determining the diagonal measurement of a block, multiply the finished block size by 1.414. This will be helpful when figuring the size of your quilt top.

Finished Block Size	Diagonal Measurement
2"	2-7/8"
2-1/2"	3-1/2"
3"	4-1/4"
3-1/2"	5"
4"	5-5/8"
4-1/2"	6-3/8"
5"	7-1/8"
5-1/2"	7-3/4"
6"	8-1/2"
6-1/2"	9-1/4"
7"	10"
7-1/2"	10-5/8"
8"	11-3/8"
8-1/2"	12"
9"	12-3/4"
9-1/2"	13-1/2"
10"	14-1/8"
10-1/2"	14-7/8"
11"	15-1/2"
11-1/2"	16-1/4"
12"	17"

SIDE-SETTING TRIANGLE BLOCKS

When determining the size of side-setting triangle blocks, multiply the finished block size by 1.414 and add 1.25" for the seam allowance.

Side-Setting Triangle Blocks	Finished Block Size
4-1/8"	2"
4-3/4"	2-1/2"
5-1/2"	3"
6-1/4"	3-1/2"
7"	4"
7-5/8"	4-1/2"
8-3/8"	5"
9-1/8"	5-1/2"
9-3/4"	6"
10-1/2"	6-1/2"
11-1/4"	7"
11-7/8"	7-1/2"
12-5/8"	8"
13-3/8"	8-1/2"
14"	9"
14-3/4"	9-1/2"
15-1/2"	10"
16-1/8"	10-1/2"
16-7/8"	11"
16-5/8"	11-1/2"
18-1/4"	12"

CORNER-SETTING TRIANGLE BLOCKS

When determining the size of corner-setting triangle blocks, divide the finished block size by 1.414 and add .875 for the seam allowance.

Corner-Setting Triangle Blocks	Finished Block Size
2-3/8"	2"
2-3/4"	2-1/2"
3"	3"
3-3/8"	3-1/2"
3-3/4"	4"
4-1/8"	4-1/2"
4-1/2"	5"
4-7/8"	5-1/2"
5-1/8"	6"
5-1/2"	6-1/2"
5-7/8"	7"
6-1/4"	7-1/2"
6-5/8"	8"
7"	8-1/2"
7-1/4"	9"
7-5/8"	9-1/2"
8"	10"
8-3/8"	10-1/2"
8-3/4"	11"
9"	11-1/2"
9-3/8"	12"

Formulas

FORMULA TO DETERMINE THE AMOUNT OF BACKING FABRIC NEEDED:

```
      ___"  (quilt top length)
+      4"   (for extra backing)
÷      36"
=      ___   yards
x      2*   (if your quilt width is 38"-80")
=      ___   yards backing fabric
(round up to nearest 1/4 yard)
```

* If your quilt width is 36" or less, multiply x1. If your quilt width is 80" or more, multiply x3.

FORMULA TO DETERMINE THE SIZE HANGING SLEEVE NEEDED:

```
      ___"  (width of quilt)
+      2"
=      ___   (length of fabric strip to cut)
```
Cut fabric strip 8"-wide x length determined above

FORMULA TO DETERMINE THE NUMBER OF BINDING STRIPS NEEDED:

```
      ___"  (top, bottom & side measurements of quilt)
+      12"   (just in case)
÷      40"   (usable fabric)
=      ___   (number of binding strips needed;
             round up if needed)
```

FORMULA TO DETERMINE THE SIZE HANGING SLEEVES NEEDED FOR A 60" OR WIDER QUILT TOP:

```
      ___"  (width of quilt)
+      2"
=      ___
÷      3     (number of hanging sleeves)
=      ___   (length of fabric strips to cut)
```
Cut three fabric strips 8"-wide x length determined above. If you choose to add more hanging sleeves, use the same formula to determine the measurements.

NUMBER OF QUARTER-SQUARE TRIANGLES FROM SPECIFIC FABRIC YARDAGE

Finished Triangle Size	Width of Strip	Fabric Yardage							
		1/4 yard	1/2 yard	3/4 yard	1 yard	1-1/4 yards	1-1/2 yards	1-3/4 yards	2 yards
2"	3-1/4"	96	240	384	528	624	768	912	1056
2-1/2"	3-3/4"	88	176	308	396	528	616	704	836
3"	4-1/4"	72	144	216	288	360	432	504	576
3-1/2"	4-3/4"	32	96	160	224	288	352	416	480
4"	5-1/4"	32	96	160	192	256	320	384	416
4-1/2"	5-3/4"	28	84	112	168	196	252	280	336
5"	6-1/4"	24	48	96	120	168	192	240	264
5-1/2"	6-3/4"	24	48	96	120	144	192	216	240
6"	7-1/4"	20	40	60	80	120	140	160	180
6-1/2"	7-3/4"	20	40	60	80	100	120	160	180
7"	8-1/4"	20	40	60	80	120	120	140	160
7-1/2"	8-3/4"	16	32	48	64	80	96	112	128
8"	9-1/4"	x	16	32	48	64	80	96	112
8-1/2"	9-3/4"	x	16	32	48	64	80	96	112
9"	10-1/4"	x	16	32	48	64	80	96	112
9-1/2"	10-3/4"	x	12	24	36	48	60	60	72
10"	11-1/4"	x	12	24	36	48	48	60	72
10-1/2"	11-3/4"	x	12	24	36	36	48	60	72
11"	12-1/4"	x	12	24	24	36	48	60	72
11-1/2"	12-3/4"	x	12	24	24	36	48	48	60
12"	13-1/4"	x	12	24	24	36	48	48	60

Number of triangles is based on 42"-long strips. Remove the selvages before cutting. A 1/4" seam allowance is included.

French-fold Binding Strips

(cut strips four times wider than the desired finished binding width and add 1/2" for seam allowances)

Desired Finished Size	Cut Strips
1/4"	1-1/2"
3/8"	2"
1/2"	2-1/2"
5/8"	3"
3/4"	3-1/2"
7/8"	4"

Triple-fold Bias Strips

(cut strips three times wider than the desired finished width of the vine or stems)

Desired Finished Size	Cut Strips
3/8"	1-1/8"
1/2"	1-1/2"
5/8"	1-7/8"
3/4"	2-1/4"
1"	3"

QUILTING TERMS & DEFINITIONS

1/4" Seam Allowance – Space between the stitched fabric seam and the raw edge

Appliqué – Adding fabric shapes to a background fabric by hand or machine

Backing – Layer of fabric on the back of a quilt

Backstitch – Stitching over one or two stitches to secure them

Basting – Securing the top, batting, and backing of a quilt with large stitches or safety pins before quilting

Batting – Layer of material between quilt top and back

Between – A short, small-eyed needle used for hand quilting

Bias – Diagonal grain of fabric that is a 45-degree angle to the selvages

Bias Strips – Strips cut at 45-degree angle on fabric's bias grain

Binding – Strip of fabric used to cover raw outer edges of a quilt

Block – Basic unit of a quilt top

Border – Fabric strips used to frame the quilt center

Chain Piecing – Sewing fabric pieces or strips in a continuous chain without backstitching or cutting the threads between pieces

Contrast – Light, medium, and dark color values

Corner Squares or Cornerstones – Squares of fabric added to sashing or border strips to align with corners of blocks or the quilt top

Crosswise Grain – Threads running perpendicular, or between, the selvages of a fabric

Cutting Mat – Mat used to protect surface when rotary cutting fabric

Diagonal Set – Quilt top setting where blocks are set-on-point in diagonal rows

Double-fold (French-fold) Binding – Fabric strip folded in half lengthwise before being sewn to quilt top

Echo Quilting – Stitching around the outside of a motif or design with multiple stitching lines expanded at regular intervals

Fabric Grain – Direction of threads in a woven fabric

Fat Eighth – 9" x 22" piece of fabric

Fat Quarter – 18" x 22" piece of fabric

Finger Pressing – Pressing fabric between fingers to make a crease

Finished Size – Measurement of completed block after being sewn in the quilt top

Flannel – 100-percent cotton fabric with a brushed, napped surface

Flying Geese Block – Rectangular block traditionally made up of three 90-degree triangles

Four-Patch Block – Block made up of four equal-size fabric squares usually in two contrasting colors

French-fold (Double-fold) Binding – Fabric strip folded in half lengthwise before being sewn to quilt top

Fusible Web – Paper-backed adhesive that is ironed to the wrong side of fabric and cut into shapes for hand or machine appliqué

Fussy Cutting – Cutting out a specific design or motif from a fabric

Half-Square Triangles – The two 90-degree triangles formed when a square is cut in half diagonally

Hand Quilting – Series of running stitches made through all quilt layers by hand with needle and thread

Hanging Sleeve – Tube of fabric sewn to back of a quilt that holds a rod so quilt can be displayed

Hourglass Block – Block made with a quarter-square triangle

Hue – Color

Lengthwise Grain – Threads running parallel to the fabric selvage; has the least amount of stretch

lof – Length of fabric

Loft – Thickness of batting

Machine Quilting – Series of stitches made through all quilt layers with a sewing machine

Marking Tools – Specialty chalks, pens, and pencils used to mark a quilt top

Mitered Border – Border strips sewn together at the corner of the quilt top at a 45-degree angle

Needle Down – Feature on some sewing machines that allows the needle to remain in the fabric when you stop sewing

Nine-Patch Block - Block made up of nine equal-size fabric squares in three rows of three squares each

Notions – Another name for quilting tools

Outline Quilting — Sewing 1/4" from a seam line or the edge of an appliqué shape

Partial Seams – Process of seaming to avoid set-in seams

Patchwork – Blocks or pieces sewn together to form a quilt top

Piecing – Sewing fabric pieces together to form a block or quilt top

Pin baste – Basting quilt top, batting, and backing together with safety pins

Pinwheel Block – Block made up of four half-square triangles sewn together to resemble a spinning pinwheel

Precuts – Fabrics cut into specific sizes or shapes; most often packaged by fabric companies to represent one fabric line; names and types of precuts differ among fabric companies

Pressing – Using the iron in an up and down motion

Quarter-Square Triangle – 90-degree triangle formed when a square is cut in half twice on the diagonal

Quilt Sandwich – The quilt top, batting, and backing layered together

Quilt Setting – Arrangement of blocks in a quilt top

Rail Fence Block – Block made up of three to four rectangles, usually of equal size

Raw Edge – Cut, unfinished edge of fabric

Rotary Cutter – Tool with a sharp, round blade used to cut fabric

Sashing – Strips of fabric sewn between blocks on a quilt top

Scale – The size of a print or pattern in a fabric

Scalloped Border – A curved border around a quilt's outer edge

Scant 1/4" Seam – one or two thread widths inside the 1/4" seam mark

Selvage – The lengthwise finished edge of the fabric

Set-on-Point - Quilt blocks that are set on the diagonal are set-on-point

Setting Block – A solid color block sewn next to a pieced block in a quilt top

Setting Triangles – Triangles used to complete a diagonal-set quilt design

Sharps – Needles with a narrow shaft and sharp point used for piecing or appliqué

Slipstitch – A hand stitch used to sew binding or appliqué to the quilt top

Stipple Quilting – An allover quilting pattern of random curved lines that resemble puzzle pieces

Stitch-in-the-Ditch – Quilting stitches sewn into or very close to the seam line

Straight Set – Blocks arranged side-by-side in a quilt top

Straightening Fabric – Straightening an edge of fabric before rotary cutting

Strip Piecing – A technique where multiple strips of fabric are sewn together and then cut into segments for blocks

Strip Set – Two or more strips of fabric sewn together the length of the strips

Subcutting – Cutting fabric into smaller units or segments

Thread Basting – Securing the quilt top, batting, and backing together with thread before quilting

Trapunto – Technique of stuffing areas of a quilt to raise a design

Unfinished Size – Size of a block before the 1/4" seam allowance has been added

Universal – Sewing machine needle used for quilting

Value – Another word for contrast

Walking Foot – A foot on your sewing machine that moves all layers of the quilt sandwich through the machine evenly

wof – Width of fabric

Zigzag Stitch – Programmed stitch on a sewing machine used for appliqué; also referred to as a satin stitch

About the Author

Currently Jeri's career has dug her deep into the process of book publishing as the Editor at Landauer Publishing. She works closely with all of Landauer's authors to ensure quality, creativity, and excellence. Her expertise and knowledge not only of publishing but of quilting has been evident throughout her entire career. Before coming to Landauer Publishing nine years ago she worked at *Fons & Porter Love of Quilting* magazine.

Jeri and her husband reside in Winterset, Iowa. They have four grown children and one granddaughter.